YORK NOTES

AQA ENGLISH LANGUAGE AND LITERATURE

WORKBOOK

STEVE EDDY

PEARSON

YORK PRESS

The right of Steve Eddy to be identified as the Author of this Work
has been asserted by him in accordance with the Copyright,
Designs and Patents Act 1988

YORK PRESS
322 Old Brompton Road, London SW5 9JH

PEARSON EDUCATION LIMITED
Edinburgh Gate, Harlow,
Essex CM20 2JE, United Kingdom
Associated companies, branches and representatives throughout the world

First published 2017

10 9 8 7 6 5

ISBN 978–1–2921–8620–7

Typeset by Carnegie Book Production
Printed in Slovakia

Text credits: 'The old debate: punish prisoners, or rehabilitate them?' © Telegraph Media Group Limited
2013. Extract from *An Inspector Calls* by J. B. Priestley (Harlow, UK: Heinemann, 1992, page 11) © J. B.
Priestley 1945. Reproduced by permission of Penguin Books Ltd, and United Agents on behalf of the
Estate of J. B. Priestley

Photo credits: Roy Pedersen/Shutterstock for page 24 / Raymond Llewellyn/Shutterstock for page 39 /
D and D Photo Sudbury/Shutterstock for page 63 / Milkovasa/Shutterstock for page 81

CONTENTS

PART ONE: THE BASICS

PART TWO: GCSE ENGLISH LANGUAGE

PART THREE: GCSE ENGLISH LITERATURE

ANSWERS

The Assessment Objectives

If you are studying the AQA course for GCSE English Language and English Literature, your work will be examined through the Assessment Objectives below.

ENGLISH LANGUAGE

AO1 to AO4 relate to the Reading sections of the exam, and AO5 and AO6 to the Writing sections:

(AO1)	• Identify and interpret explicit and implicit information and ideas. • Select and synthesise evidence from different texts.
(AO2)	Explain, comment on and analyse how writers use language and structure to achieve effects and influence readers, using relevant subject terminology to support their views.
(AO3)	Compare writers' ideas and perspectives, as well as how these are conveyed, across two or more texts.
(AO4)	Evaluate texts critically and support this with appropriate textual references.
(AO5)	• Communicate clearly, effectively and imaginatively, selecting and adapting tone, style and register for different forms, purposes and audiences. • Organise information and ideas, using structural and grammatical features to support coherence and cohesion of texts.
(AO6)	Use a range of vocabulary and sentence structures for clarity, purpose and effect, with accurate spelling and punctuation. (20% of total marks)

ENGLISH LITERATURE

(AO1)	Read, understand and respond to texts. Students should be able to: • maintain a critical style and develop an informed personal response • use textual references, including quotations, to support and illustrate interpretations.
(AO2)	Analyse the language, form and structure used by a writer to create meanings and effects, using relevant subject terminology where appropriate.
(AO3)	Show understanding of the relationships between texts and the contexts in which they were written.
(AO4)	Use a range of vocabulary and sentence structures, for clarity, purpose and effect, with accurate spelling and punctuation.

Look out for the AO labels throughout this Workbook to help keep you on track.

: The basics: Spelling, punctuation and grammar

A06 **A04**

TOP TIP

It is important to make sure that you spell words correctly. Spelling rules can help you remember spellings that you find difficult. Use the tasks below to test and practise your spellings.

PRACTISE YOUR SKILLS

PLURALS

27/12/19

❶ Give the correct **plurals** for the following words:

a) belief ...*s*... cherry ...*cherries*... chief ...*chiefs*... church*es*...

b) cuff *s*... dairy ...*diarys*... donkey ...*donkeys*... fairy ...*fairies*...

c) fox ...*s*... glass ...*es*... journey ...*s*... scarf ...*scarves*...

d) knife ...*knives*... lorry ...*s*... monkey ...*s*... peach ...*es*...

e) ruff ...*s*... tray ...*s*... wharf ...*s*... wolf ...*s*...

PREFIXES AND SUFFIXES

27/12/19

❷ Give the correct **spellings**, using **prefixes** (e.g. *ir*, *un*, *in*), for the **opposites** of these words:

a) acceptable .... regular .... necessary .... polite ....

b) intelligent ...*un*... caring ...*un*... efficient ...*in*... eligible ....

c) precise .... appropriate .... edible .... equal ....

❸ The words *breakable* and *edible* use the **suffixes** *able* and *ible*. Use the correct **suffix** to create words that mean:

a) easily noticed ...*noticible*...   27/12/19

b) easily accessed ...*accesable*...

c) easily managed ....

d) able to be read (of handwriting) ...*legible*...

e) easily excited ....

f) able to be divided ....

❹ Correct the following: 27/12/19

allways .... beautifuly .... allmost ....

hopefull .... impresive .... beautifull ....

pennyless .... untill .... worrysome ....

HOMOPHONES

To do 27/12/19

❺ Circle the correct **spellings** in this piece of writing:

✓

When I went to see the [principal / ~~principle~~], she said she would [right / write] me a letter on her own [stationary / stationery] so that I [wood / would] be [aloud / allowed] to miss Games.

'[Its / It's] not often I do this,' she said. '[It's / Its] a question of [principal / principle]. I only do it for someone [whose / who's] got a genuine excuse – for example, [their / there] health is poor and [there / they're] in danger of it getting worse. I don't know [whether / weather] you realise that. Anyway, [its / it's] [too / two] late for Games now, so this letter may have already lost [it's / its] usefulness.'

As I walked to the changing rooms, I felt relieved. My excuse had been [accepted / excepted]. Everything was fine – [accept / except] that I couldn't think [where / wear] the letter had got to!

DIFFICULT SPELLINGS

❻ Check that you know the following **spellings**. Split the word into syllables to help you remember. Test yourself using the 'Look, Say, Cover, Write, Check' method.

accommodation	exhilarating	*government*
acquit	humorous	
appearance	liaison	*realistic*
circumstances	manoeuvre	*accumulate*
committed	occurrence	*peril*
definitely	playwright	*jeopardy*
dilemma	schedule	
embarrass	unconscious	

PROGRESS LOG [tick the correct box]   Needs more work ☐   Getting there ☐   Under control ☐

Sentences and grammar

TOP TIP

Make sure that you write grammatically correct sentences and vary your use of sentence types for effect.

Remember:

- All sentences contain a main verb and a subject.
- Complex sentences contain at least one main clause and a subordinate clause.
- Minor or incomplete sentences can be used, but only sparingly.

PRACTISE YOUR SKILLS

SENTENCE TYPES

❶ Rewrite the following pairs of **simple** sentences as single **complex** ones, i.e. use relative pronouns such as 'which', 'who', and/or conjunctions.

a) *Aled is a plumber by trade. He is very practical.* ....

....

b) *Aberdeen is a long way north. It gets very cold in winter.* ....

....

c) *I was brought up in Calcutta. It is a huge city.* ....

....

❷ Turn each of these **complex** sentences into two **simple** ones:

a) *Having bought a ticket, she felt she might as well go to the concert.* ....

....

b) *Amir, who preferred football to Maths, stayed away.* ....

....

c) *I scored once, which is more than Wayne ever manages.* ....

....

❸ Rewrite these sentences to include a **minor sentence** for dramatic effect:

a) *I opened the safe, but it was empty.* ....

....

b) *It was silent, apart from the beating of my heart.* ....

....

c) *There was nothing but rain all day.* ....

....

❹ Rewrite this student's paragraph using a range of **different sentence types**. Add any words you need to make it flow.

> I rushed to the river. I jumped in. I swam across. The water was freezing. It took my breath away as if it had been sucked out of me. I made it to the other side. I just had time to look back. They were still pursuing me. I saw a puff of smoke from a rifle. I heard a crack like a branch breaking. I heard a bullet ricochet off the rocks a foot away from me. I put my head down and ran.

....

....

....

....

....

CLAUSES

❺ Underline the **noun clauses** (dependent clauses acting as nouns):
   a) We can have whatever we want.
   b) Give the prize to whoever arrives first.
   c) What you see is what you get.

❻ Underline the **relative clauses** (clauses adding information to the main clause):
   a) Fatima, who lives in Peckham, had to take the bus.
   b) We watched *Peaky Blinders*, which is set in Birmingham.
   c) China, which has a fast-growing economy, objected.

❼ Underline the **adverbial clauses** (dependent clauses that modify a main clause):
   a) You'll need a thermal jacket if you're going to avoid freezing.
   b) To stalk the seal, the polar bear swims underwater.
   c) I'm going to let you off this time because of your previous good behaviour.

VERBS

❽ Circle the correct **verb form**. Remember: **subject** and **verb** must 'agree'.
   a) The runners [was / were] approaching the finish.
   b) A flock of sheep [has / have] wandered on to the road.
   c) The wolf pack [is / are] hunting a bison.

❾ Replace the underlined words with the correct form of the conditional tense:
   a) What would you say if I <u>sing</u> .... out of tune?
   b) If I <u>was</u> .... to complain, I would only annoy them.
   c) If I <u>buy</u> .... these jeans now, would you change them if necessary?

PROGRESS LOG [tick the correct box] Needs more work ☐ Getting there ☐ Under control ☐

Punctuation

TOP TIP

Using punctuation accurately and creatively will help you convey meaning, while varying your punctuation can add interest.

PRACTISE YOUR SKILLS

COMMAS AND FULL STOPS

❶ Add **commas** to make the meaning of these sentences clear:
   a) After eating Kevin Ian and Ravi went to the park.
   b) Malachi who is doing Media Studies directed the video.
   c) Sue who works in Boots came to the party but Sue who's in our class didn't.

❷ Add **commas** where necessary to these listing sentences:
   a) Rain snow and sleet along with black ice are some of the road hazards today.
   b) The current stars of *TOWIE Coronation Street* and *EastEnders* and a few from *Emmerdale Hollyoaks* and *Home and Away* attended the event.
   c) She ordered a sandwich with salmon cream cheese and cucumber and waited.

❸ Which two of these lines are **correctly punctuated**? Tick the boxes.
   a) Eva drank her coffee immediately, she hated it cold. ☑
   b) Bread needs to rise. You can't make it in five minutes. ☐
   c) France is twice the size of Britain, it has more space. ☑
   d) Britain has a queen: it is technically a monarchy. ☐

COLONS AND SEMICOLONS   to do with all.

❹ Which of these are functions of the **colon**? Tick one or more boxes.
   a) Introducing a list ☐
   b) Dividing items in a list ☐
   c) Announcing an explanation or elaboration of a point ☐
   d) Expressing surprise ☐

❺ Add **colons** and/or **semicolons** to the following sentences:
   a) There is only one reason to shop at Betterbuy it's cheap.
   b) Dogs are obedient, loving and loyal cats will cuddle up to anyone who feeds them.
   c) We took the following ropes, flexible ladders and clips sandwiches, drinks and snacks and a range of maps.

6 Insert **dashes** in the following sentences:

a) Egypt with the Nile, tombs and pyramids is one of the most popular destinations.

b) I have one relative a cousin, but I last saw him two years ago.

c) You of all people should understand.

7 Add **commas** and **speech marks** to the following dialogue:

a) Desiree he insisted is the only girl for me.

b) Once upon a time I began there was a little girl called Goldilocks.

c) I stared hard at him. Who do you think you're fooling? I said. Not me, for one.

8 Add **parentheses** (round brackets like these) to these sentences:

a) My great-grandfather drove a Centurion a kind of tank in the war.

b) I listed the things I needed: flour plain, sugar brown, butter or margarine and a lemon.

c) Panamanians most of them are Spanish-speaking.

9 Add the **correct punctuation**, including capital letters where necessary, in the following passage.

> It was a sunny afternoon in the park James Darrel and Omar were kicking a ball around Emma and Sita were sitting on the grass texting
>
> Emma looked up from her phone when a buzzing noise distracted her she thought at first it was a large bee she hated bees having been stung once
>
> Sita heard it too what's that she said looking around that buzzing
>
> The boys had stopped their game though it had hardly been a proper game in the first place there were only three of them
>
> Look said Darrel pointing up it's a tiny spaceship
>
> Don't be daft said Omar I'll tell you what it is a drone they're being used to deliver parcels now
>
> Well do you really think that one's delivering a parcel said Darrel I think it's spying on us probably scouting for new talent

CHAPTER 2: Paper 1, Section A: Reading fiction

Identifying information

PAPER 1,
SECTION A, Q1

EXAM BASICS

What you have to do:

- List four pieces of information about an aspect of a short section of a source provided – such as the weather, or a character.

Remember:

- You can list information that is made explicit (stated) or that is implied (hinted at).
- Stick to the given section and aspect.
- You can quote (if the meaning is very clear) or paraphrase (put the information in your own words).

PRACTISE YOUR SKILLS

EXPLICIT INFORMATION   (obvious)

Read this passage from *The Remarkable Case of Davidson's Eyes*, by H. G. Wells, and the task below it. Bellows, the narrator, is describing what happened to his colleague, Davidson.

> When I say that I was the immediate witness of his seizure, I mean that I was the first on the scene. The thing happened at the Harlow Technical College, just beyond the Highgate Archway. He was alone in the larger laboratory when the thing happened. I was in a smaller room, where the balances are, writing up some notes. The thunderstorm had completely upset my work, of course. It was just after one of the louder peals that I thought I heard some glass smash in the other room. I stopped writing, and turned round to listen. For a moment I heard nothing; the hail was playing the devil's tattoo on the corrugated zinc of the roof. Then came another sound, a smash – no doubt of it this time. Something heavy had been knocked off the bench.

Task: List four pieces of explicit information from this text about what the narrator remembers.

❶ Read the answers one student gave to this task:

a) Bellows saw the first moment of Davidson's seizure.

b) Bellows was a student.

c) A thunderstorm broke a window.

d) The hail made a loud noise as it hit the metal roof.

On a separate piece of paper, identify which of these answers is correct, and explain why the others are wrong.

❷ Now find **four** other pieces of explicit information about what the
narrator remembers from the extract on page 12: *sentences please*

a) *Bell oaks was the first to arrive after Davidson had a seizure.*

b) *The incident happened at Harlow Technical College.*

c) *He was alone when he had a seizure.*

d)

IMPLICIT INFORMATION *(implies)*

Read this further extract about Bellows's encounter with Davidson.

> I jumped up at once and went and opened the door leading into the big laboratory.
>   I was surprised to hear a queer sort of laugh, and saw Davidson standing unsteadily in the middle
> of the room, with a dazzled look on his face. My first impression was that he was drunk. He did not
> notice me. He was clawing out at something invisible a yard in front of his face. He put out his
> hand, slowly, rather hesitatingly, and then clutched nothing. 'What's come to it?' he said. He held
> up his hands to his face, fingers spread out. 'Great Scott!' he said.

❸ What can we **infer** about Davidson? Note down **four** things. For example:
'Something extremely powerful happened to him ...'. *infers sentences please*

a) *He is confused because he has a "dazzled look".*

b) *Bellows Davidson He thinks he can't see because the text says, "clawing at something invisible."*

c) *He wants to see it he can see his own hands*

d) *Davidson did not notice Bellows.*

PARAPHRASING *to do with me*

❹ **Paraphrase** the following sentence and phrase, showing that you understand their meaning. Write in the **present tense**.

a) 'My first impression was that he was drunk.' Start:
He appears to be ~~it~~ intoxicated.

b) 'and then clutched nothing.' Start:
He grabbed the air,

TEST YOUR UNDERSTANDING

❺ Read this further passage from the story.

He looked round him in every direction. 'I could swear that was Bellows. Why don't you show yourself like a man, Bellows?'

It occurred to me that he must be suddenly struck blind. I walked round the table and laid my hand upon his arm. I never saw a man more startled in my life. He jumped away from me, and came round into an attitude of self-defence, his face fairly distorted with terror. 'Good God!' he cried. 'What was that?'

'It's I – Bellows. Confound it, Davidson!'

He jumped when I answered him and stared – how can I express it? – right through me. He began talking, not to me, but to himself. 'Here in broad daylight on a clear beach. Not a place to hide in.' He looked about him wildly. 'Here! I'm off.' He suddenly turned and ran headlong into the big electro-magnet.

List **four** pieces of information we find out about Davidson and his situation. These can be **direct details**, or things that are **implied**.

a) ....

....

....

b) ....

....

....

c) ....

....

....

d) ....

....

....

PROGRESS LOG [tick the correct box]   Needs more work ☐   Getting there ☐   Under control ☐

Analysing language features

A02

PAPER 1,
SECTION A, Q2

EXAMBASICS

What you have to do:

- Answer a question about a particular aspect from a section of the source you have been given (about ten lines).
- Write about how the writer's use of language creates particular effects.

Remember:

- Focus on that aspect alone (e.g. the weather, a person, the setting).
- Choose short, appropriate quotations.
- Concentrate on the effect of the language.

PRACTISE YOUR SKILLS

WORDS AND PHRASES

Read this short text from *Wuthering Heights* in which the narrator gazes through a window into another house.

PETER

> [It] was beautiful – a splendid place carpeted with crimson, and crimson-covered chairs and tables, and a pure white ceiling bordered with gold, a shower of glass-drops hanging in silver chains from the centre, and shimmering with little soft tapers.

❶ How does the writer use **words and phrases** here to describe the **effect** of the room on the narrator?

- Circle any words **describing the room**.
- Note down **their effect** on the narrator. (How does he or she feel as a result of seeing this?) Continue on a separate sheet of paper if necessary.

....

....

....

❷ Read this paragraph from a different text.

> The boy watched, transfixed, as his father raised the sword in the air. It gleamed and shone, and his mouth gaped as the edge caught the light and momentarily sent a flash of white across the room. Oh, how he wished to hold that sword, to weave spells with it. But it was forbidden. Not for children.

Now read this response by one student about the effect on the boy of seeing the sword. He or she has forgotten to add any quotations to support the point made. Rewrite the response, adding **at least two quotations**.

> The boy responds to seeing the sword as if it is something magical. He is utterly amazed by its appearance. Together these descriptions suggest a world that hypnotises him.

....

....

....

....

USE OF SENTENCES

❸ What is notable about the **final two sentences** of the text about the sword?

....

....

❹ What **effect** do they create?

....

....

LANGUAGE TECHNIQUES

Look at this box containing different language techniques. Can you remember what each one is?

punctuation for impact	pattern of three	simile	sibilance	metaphor
repetition	onomatopoeia		alliteration	

❺ Which of these **language techniques** can you identify in the passage from *Wuthering Heights* below? Write any relevant letters against the words/ phrases in the paragraph.

> *Pray, don't imagine that he conceals depths of benevolence and affection beneath a stern exterior! He's not a rough diamond – a pearl-containing oyster of a rustic: he's a fierce, pitiless, wolfish man! … [He'd] crush you like a sparrow's egg.*

❻ Now, complete this paragraph:

In this passage, Heathcliff is presented as a violent character who ....

....

It also suggests that Isabella mustn't be deceived into thinking he is ....

....

....

TEST YOUR UNDERSTANDING

❼ Read this longer paragraph from *Wuthering Heights*. In it, Heathcliff has just learned of the death of his lover, Catherine.

Oh, God! it is unutterable! I cannot live without my life! I cannot live without my soul!'
He dashed his head against the knotted trunk; and, lifting up his eyes, howled, not like a man, but like a savage beast being goaded to death with knives and spears. I observed several splashes of blood about the bark of the tree, and his hand and forehead were both stained; probably the scene I witnessed was a repetition of others acted during the night. It hardly moved my compassion – it appalled me: still, I felt reluctant to quit him so. But the moment he recollected himself enough to notice me watching, he thundered a command for me to go, and I obeyed. He was beyond my skill to quiet or console!

How does the writer use language here to describe the effect of Catherine's death on Heathcliff? You could comment on **words and phrases**, **language features** and **sentence forms**.

....

....

....

....

....

....

....

....

....

....

....

....

....

....

....

....

....

....

....

....

....

PROGRESS LOG [tick the correct box]   Needs more work ☐   Getting there ☐   Under control ☐

Understanding structures

EXAM BASICS

What you have to do:

- Write about the structure of the whole source provided.
- Identify the writer's focus, and how and why it changes as the source develops.
- Comment on other structural features you notice.

Remember:

- Think about the overall structure – and how specific words, phrases and sentences contribute to it.
- Look for structural elements or devices such as contrasts, or sequencing (e.g. flashback).
- Look for change or development, such as a shift in the writer's focus, or increasing tension.

PRACTISE YOUR SKILLS

OPENINGS

Read the two fiction openings below, then answer the questions that follow.

> A. *Let the reader be introduced to Lady Carbury, upon whose character and doings much will depend of whatever interest these pages may have, as she sits at her writing-table in her own room in her own house in Welbeck Street. Lady Carbury spent many hours at her desk, and wrote many letters – wrote also very much beside letters.*
>
> Anthony Trollope, *The Way We Live Now*
>
> B. *Day had broken cold and gray, exceedingly cold and gray, when the man turned aside from the main Yukon trail and climbed the high earth-bank, where a dim and little-travelled trail led eastward through the fat spruce timberland.*
>
> Jack London, 'To Build a Fire'

❶ Which **opening** gains the **reader's interest** by:

a) addressing the reader?

b) giving a strong sense of setting?

c) raising questions about a character's daily life?

d) raising questions as to why a character is where they are?

THE ELEMENTS OF STRUCTURE

❷ Which of these are important **elements of structure**? Tick one or more boxes.

a) sequencing ☑

b) use of commas ☐

c) 'zooming in' from an overall view to a detail ☑

d) scene-setting ☑

e) alliteration ☐

f) narrative viewpoint ☐

g) similes ☐

h) connections between paragraphs ☑

i) topic sentences ☑

j) word choices ☐

❸ Which of the elements of structure listed in Task 2 are used in the following passage? Identify **how structure is used** in each of the underlined sections. The first one has been done for you.

> *He crouched behind the bin and scanned the view: <u>an expanse of wet concrete, and behind it a railway viaduct over six red-brick arches, each sealed to form an individual lock-up. Beneath a sign reading 'JD Engines Ltd' was a solid steel gate. In this gate, a door was inset.</u>*[a] *Any moment now, that door <u>would fly open.</u>*[b]
>
> *<u>Yesterday it had all been different.</u>*[c] *He had been a free man. That was before Arthur had approached him about 'a little job'.*
> *<u>Suddenly a gunshot sounded and Arthur burst out running.</u>*[d]

a) *The passage follows the man's view, focusing in on the door.*

b) it makes the reader want to know why the door will fly open and or what will emerge

c) it uses a flashback and identifies the point in time that led directly to the mans present predicment

d) it returns to the present moment – litterally

TEST YOUR UNDERSTANDING

❹ Read this passage from *To the Lighthouse*, by Virginia Woolf, in which a family are in a sailing boat.

The rush of the water ceased; the world became full of little creaking and squeaking sounds. One heard the waves breaking and flapping against the side of the boat as if they were anchored in harbour. Everything became very close to one. For the sail, upon which James had his eyes fixed until it had become to him like a person whom he knew, sagged entirely; there they came to a stop, flapping about waiting for a breeze, in the hot sun, miles from shore, miles from the Lighthouse. Everything in the whole world seemed to stand still. The Lighthouse became immovable, and the line of the distant shore became fixed. The sun grew hotter and everybody seemed to come very close together and to feel each other's presence, which they had almost forgotten. Macalister's fishing line went plumb down into the sea. But Mr Ramsay went on reading with his legs curled under him.

How has the writer **structured this text** so it interests the reader?

The passage begins with the sense of hearing, describing sounds as the wind drops, it then shifts to the sight of the sail from James viewpoint and the boat being ~~crossed out~~ still, everything stops, and the people in the boat become more aware.

Evaluating characters, themes and settings

A04

PAPER 1,
SECTION A, Q4

EXAM BASICS

What you have to do:

- Decide how far you agree with a statement about an aspect of the source.
- Evaluate the source critically, with textual evidence.

Remember:

- Focus on the statement and the aspect of the source it identifies.
- Stick to the specified section of the source.
- Provide evidence, and analyse and evaluate it.

PRACTISE YOUR SKILLS

CHARACTERISATION THROUGH APPEARANCE

Read this description of Count Dracula in Bram Stoker's *Dracula*.

> *His face was a strong – a very strong – aquiline,[1] with high bridge of the thin nose and peculiarly arched nostrils; with lofty domed forehead, and hair growing scantily round the temples but profusely elsewhere. His eyebrows were very massive, almost meeting over the nose, and with bushy hair that seemed to curl in its own profusion. The mouth, so far as I could see it under the heavy moustache, was fixed and rather cruel-looking, with peculiarly sharp white teeth; these protruded over the lips, whose remarkable ruddiness showed astonishing vitality in a man of his years. For the rest, his ears were pale, and at the tops extremely pointed; the chin was broad and strong, and the cheeks firm though thin. The general effect was one of extraordinary pallor.*
>
> *[His hands were] rather coarse – broad, with squat fingers. Strange to say, there were hairs in the centre of the palm. The nails were long and fine, and cut to a sharp point.*
>
> [1]*aquiline – like an eagle*

❶ Draw lines to match the **details** and **word choices** on the right to the impression they create of the Count. The first one has been done for you.

a) physically strong and healthy — 'massive' eyebrows; 'cruel-looking' mouth

b) strong-willed and decisive — 'sharp white teeth; nails 'cut to a sharp point'

c) ghostly, or connected to death — 'hairs in the centre of the palm'

d) threatening or menacing — 'lips whose remarkable ruddiness showed astonishing vitality'

e) unnatural — 'extraordinary pallor'

f) a vampire — 'a strong […] aquiline'; 'the chin was broad and strong'

CHARACTERISATION THROUGH ACTION AND SPEECH

Read this extract about a character called Anton eating breakfast in a café with his wife.

> *Anton folded his arms tightly and glared at his plate.*
> *'That's not what I ordered,' he told his wife, starting to gesture impatiently towards the retreating waitress. 'Why can't the idiots in these places get anything right? I specifically requested poached eggs, plural, on white toast. What do they bring me?'*
> *'Don't make a fuss, dear,' she pleaded.*
> *He snorted, ripped open a butter pat, stabbed it with his knife, and squashed it hard onto the toast, scraping it to each corner. He paused to scowl at his wife before sawing off a mouthful.*

❷ Write your answers to the questions below on a separate piece of paper:

    a) How do the writer's **verb choices** effectively suggest Anton's character?

    b) How does the writer convey Anton's **character** by **what he does and says**?

CHARACTER AND THEMES

Read this passage from a text about a homeless person called Ellie.

> *Ellie huddled against the wall, hugging threadbare knees, her freezing fingers holding out a plastic cup. All these people passing by on the busy street had places to go: glossy jobs in glass-fronted offices; lunch dates with eager friends in cosy bars; heated homes with thick-piled carpets and big TVs. Her? Empty pockets, boots with holes, ripped jacket. She shivered.*
> *'Spare change?' she mumbled as a woman in an elegant mohair coat and glinting jewellery clicked past on strappy heels. The woman glanced away, suddenly interested in something across the road. That was when she knew it – she was invisible, like a ghost sensed only by dogs and children. The passers-by saw only a bundle of rags with an empty cup.*

❸ How does the writer successfully use the **language techniques** below to explore the theme of being **an outsider**?

    a) listing   **d)** revealing details

    b) short and incomplete sentences   **e)** different viewpoints

    c) contrast

❹ Complete this student's evaluation:

The details describing Ellie's .... lighting ....
.... show how poor she is. Her state is effectively contrasted with
that of the ....
.... When the woman glances away, she is probably ....
.... The simile comparing Ellie to a ....
shows how ....

SETTING AND ATMOSPHERE

❺ Which of these lines from different short stories relate to **setting**? Tick
one or more boxes.

a) 'Around the turn of the century ...' ☐

b) 'The train came clanking along ...' ☐

c) 'Forcing their way through tangled undergrowth ...' ☐

d) 'No one', she said grimly, 'will dare to defy me.' ☐

e) 'The sun hung overhead, blazing down on the baked sand.' ☐

f) 'Shelves of leather-bound volumes stretched as far as
she could see.' ☐

g) 'His smiling eyes formed tiny creases.' ☐

❻ Fill in the blanks in these statements about **setting** and how it can be
used by authors. Use the list of options below:

a) Helps to create an appropriate .... – such as tense, relaxed,
menacing.

b) Prepares the reader for a particular sort of ....

c) Helps the reader to .... where the action takes place.

d) Can be associated with a major .... – e.g. Dracula and his castle.

e) Can include place, time of day and ....

| action | character | describe | imagine | metaphor | mood | weather |

❼ Read this further passage from *Dracula*.

> *Never did tombs look so ghastly white; never did cypress, or yew, or
> juniper so seem the embodiment of funereal gloom; never did tree or
> grass wave or rustle so ominously; never did bough creak so
> mysteriously; and never did the far-away howling of dogs send such a
> woeful presage[1] through the night.*
>
> *[...] He pointed; and far down the avenue of yews we saw a white
> figure advance – a dim white figure, which held something dark at its
> breast. The figure stopped, and at the moment a ray of moonlight fell
> upon the masses of driving clouds and showed in startling prominence a
> dark-haired woman, dressed in the cerements[2] of the grave.*
>
> [1]*presage* – omen, warning
> [2]*cerements* – burial shroud

A student has been asked to evaluate how well the **setting** above creates
a sense of **menace**. On a separate piece of paper, rewrite the student's
response, adding **evidence**, with whatever words you need to weave it in.

> The setting creates a sense of menace, particularly the tombs and gloomy trees. Even the
> sounds of nature and the dogs seem threatening. This prepares us for the frightening
> moment when the woman appears. The description makes this dramatic.

USING POINT, EVIDENCE, ANALYSIS – AND EVALUATION

Read the following passage and answer the questions that follow.

> *Aaron's dark eyes darted around his kingdom. He leapt, cat-like, from one mound of twisted metal to another, peering into shadows, turning over likely-looking sheets of chipboard, pausing to pick up an object and either toss it away or tuck it into his sack.*
>
> *The smell of rotting domesticity, damp and decay that hung on the air was to Aaron the perfume of possibility. This tumbled heap of dripping detritus was his treasure trove.*
>
> *'Over here!' he called to Fliss, who was surveying the scene with distaste, arms folded, standing determinedly on the perimeter of the dump. A derelict mattress flopped over like an exhausted overweight runner only made her think of her own comfortable bed.*
>
> *'Whoah!' he exclaimed. 'There's a whole pile of electrical stuff – toasters, radios, the lot. Think of the copper wire!' He knelt on a sodden carpet and began an eager examination of each appliance.*

❽ Which do you think is the writer's main **purpose**? Tick the correct box.

a) To highlight the need for recycling ☐

b) To disgust the reader ☐

c) To show Aaron's character ☐

d) To show that Fliss is fussy ☐

❾ Use colour coding to identify the **Point, Evidence and Analysis** in this paragraph.

> Fliss does not share Aaron's enthusiasm. Her 'surveying the scene with distaste', her 'folded' arms and her remaining 'on the perimeter' all indicate her refusal to get involved.

❿ Rewrite the paragraph, **varying the order** of the Point, Evidence and Analysis, and adding an Evaluation. For example, you could now begin with Evidence.

....

....

....

....

....

....

....

....

....

TEST YOUR UNDERSTANDING

⑪ Read this task, which refers to the passage on the previous page.

A reviewer has written:

'This passage is very effective in showing what an enthusiastic opportunist Aaron is.'

To what extent do you agree?

Write at least **two paragraphs** in response. Make sure you:

- Consider your **own impressions** of Aaron.
- Evaluate how the writer conveys Aaron's **character**.
- Support your response with **references from the text**.

TER 3: Paper 1, Section B: Writing descriptive and narrative texts

Describing setting and creating atmosphere

PAPER 1, SECTION B

EXAM BASICS

What you have to do:

- For Paper 1, Section B you will be asked to write a story, part of a story or an imaginative description. Describing setting and creating atmosphere is a key part of this task.

Remember:

- Choose details that serve your narrative or descriptive purpose.
- Use interesting and effective descriptive language.
- Do not overdescribe (e.g. using three adjectives when one would do equally well).

PRACTISE YOUR SKILLS

DECIDE ON THE EFFECT YOU WANT TO ACHIEVE

1 Imagine you are writing a **description** of a beach, as a story setting or simply as a piece of descriptive writing. Read the descriptions of **atmospheres** below:

a) Relaxed, lazy, exotic – perhaps a character is enjoying a dream holiday

b) Busy, bustling, lively, fun – could be a family outing

c) Bleak, lonely, melancholy – either just a description, or a character walking and mourning the loss of happier times

Indicate which atmosphere you think is the best match for each of the details below by writing a, b or c in the boxes.

biting east wind ☐ coconut palms ☐ beach balls ☐ deckchairs jammed together ☐

hypnotic sound of surf ☐ shingle ☐ rock pools with starfish ☐ jagged rocks ☐

inflatables ☐ melting ice cream ☐ gentle breeze ☐ tide-ribbed sand ☐

looming clouds ☐ pelicans flying overhead ☐ sandcastles ☐

CHOOSING VERBS *Hmwk*

❷ Underline the most **interesting** and/or **appropriate verb**:

a) The cold east wind [goes / gets / <u>slices</u> / pushes] right through her thin jacket.

b) Pelicans [<u>flapped</u> / zoomed / flew / fluttered] lazily over the blue lagoon.

c) In the storm, huge waves [<u>dashed</u> / splashed / billowed / fractured] against the jagged rocks.

d) It was a perfect day for relaxing on the beach. A faint breeze [shook / agitated / <u>fanned</u> / bent] the coconut palms.

CHOOSING ADJECTIVES *Hmwk*

❸ Underline the most **powerful** and/or **appropriate adjective**:

a) The dungeon was dark and felt unhealthily [horrid / freezing / unpleasant / <u>dank</u>] after the fresh summer air outside.

b) Jungle creepers coil round the trees like [long / <u>writhing</u> / confused / dangly] snakes.

c) A fresh layer of [<u>powdery</u> / flimsy / dusty / white] snow lay on the ground.

d) She needed to get above the flood, but the walls of the tower were [high / towering / <u>unscalable</u> / lanky].

USING IMAGERY

❹ Rewrite this passage, replacing the underlined phrases with more **effective imagery**.

> The river <u>semicircled</u> around the promontory, lapping like <u>some sort of animal</u> at its slippery banks. When tourist boats passed, they seemed to the villagers as big as <u>centres of population on the water</u>. At nights their lights shone like <u>big, bright, shiny things</u>, seeming to offer a <u>big pile of possible riches</u>. By day, the villagers rowed out in tiny boats, <u>small, crawling, water insects</u> on the face of the river, to sell rolls of cloth. Often the tourists would ignore them, gazing across at the <u>general messiness of jungle</u> on the far bank.

The river ~~y~~ turned around the promontory, lapping like a cheetah at its slippery banks. When tourist boats passed they seemed to the villagers as big as ~~centres of populat~~ *a ~~star~~ floating islands*. on At nights their lights shone like big, bright, shiny things, seeming to offer a ~~big~~ *gigantic* glass of riches. By ~~day~~ the villagers rowed out in tiny boats, ~~small,~~ *miniscule* bugs on the ~~ice~~ of the river, to sell rolls of cloth. Often the tourists would ignore them, gazing across at the general ~~mess~~ ~~uncleaness of~~ ~~a~~ tress on the far bank.

USING REPETITION

Read this description of setting, by Charles Dickens in *Bleak House*, in which he creates an atmosphere of dreary corruption:

> *Fog everywhere. Fog up the river, where it flows among green aits[1] and meadows; fog down the river, where it rolls defiled[2] among the tiers of shipping and the waterside pollutions of a great (and dirty) city. Fog on the Essex marshes, fog on the Kentish heights. Fog creeping into the cabooses[3] of collier-brigs;[4] fog lying out on the yards and hovering in the rigging of great ships; fog drooping on the gunwales[5] of barges and small boats. Fog in the eyes and throats of ancient Greenwich pensioners, wheezing by the firesides of their wards; fog in the stem and bowl of the afternoon pipe of the wrathful skipper, down in his close cabin.*

[1]*aits* – islands
[2]*defiled* – corrupted, made dirty
[3]*cabooses* – cabins
[4]*collier-brigs* – coal boats
[5]*gunwales* – upper edges of a boat's sides

❺ On a separate piece of paper, write a paragraph of your own using repetition like this. Begin with one of the following:

- *Rain everywhere …*
- *Snow everywhere …*
- *The sun blazing down on everything …*

TEST YOUR UNDERSTANDING

❻ Write a **description** of a beach, a river scene or an urban landscape, either as a story setting or for a piece of descriptive writing. Decide on the **atmosphere** you want to create. Include:

- Well-chosen details
- Vivid and interesting verbs and adjectives
- Some imagery
- Some repetition for effect

....

....

....

....

....

....

....

....

....

Creating characters

PAPER 1, SECTION B

EXAM BASICS

What you have to do:

- For this question, you might choose to write a character-based narrative or a character description.

Remember:

- 'Show, don't tell' – reveal characters through appearance, speech and actions, and how others react to them.
- Choose details to create a sense of character.
- Be consistent – avoid contradictory details.

PRACTISE YOUR SKILLS

USING APPEARANCE TO SUGGEST CHARACTER

Hmwt 20/1/2020

❶ Read the **characteristics** below (a, b, c, d) followed by the **descriptions**. Think about which descriptions best suit each characteristic, then match them by writing a, b, c or d in the boxes.

   a) feels appearance is important, likes to be in authority

   b) thinks a great deal about issues, has strong views

   c) relaxed, likes company, seems happy

   d) shy, nervous in company

clothes neat, shoes polished ☐   furrowed brow ☐   says little ☐   speaks quietly ☐

smiles a great deal ☐   rarely makes eye contact ☐   upright posture ☐

leans forward to listen to others ☐   taps to music ☐   holds hands behind back ☐

presses fingertips together ☐   leans back in chair ☐   rests chin on hand ☐

WHAT CHARACTERS SAY

Hmwk 20/1/2020

❷ What do these lines **suggest** about the **speaker**?

   a) 'You people are all the same.' *This speaker seems to be* ....

   ....

   b) 'I want all this spotless – in an hour.' *This speaker seems to be* ....

   ....

   c) 'If you don't say something now, I'm going to scream!' *This speaker seems to be* ....

   ....

USING ACTIONS TO CONVEY CHARACTER OR MOOD

❸ Draw a line to match each **action** to a **character** description:

Hmmh 20/1

Action

Character

a) He sat back from the desk, fingers laced behind his head, one leg hanging over the other, observing his visitor.

Bullying, aggressive, angry

Relaxed, confident, dominant

b) She checks her watch: 15.46. Slipping off the safety catch, gun held vertical in both hands, she edges along the rooftop.

Anxious, uneasy, unconfident or tense

Efficient, cool, collected, professional

c) She smoothed down her skirt, fiddled with her necklace as if it were too tight, and glanced towards the door.

d) He seized Alfie's collar, hoisted him off the ground, and glared, lips curled into a snarl.

MOTIVATION – WHAT CHARACTERS WANT

Hmmh

❹ What do you think is the main **motivation** of each of these characters?

a) He gazed longingly at the boss's sleek BMW. *One day*, he thought, *one day*.

....

....

b) 'Do you like this dress?' she asked. 'I chose it specially.' She placed the plate of food before him. 'Look – your favourite.'

....

....

c) When she became president, no one would dare refuse her anything!

....

....

❺ Write a similar sentence **describing a character**, or **from the viewpoint of a character**, expressing their **motivation**.

....

....

....

....

Hurst

USING A FIRST-PERSON NARRATOR

In this passage the narrator tells the story but also reveals his own character.

> *It is impossible to say how first the idea entered my brain; but once conceived, it haunted me day and night. Object there was none. Passion there was none. I loved the old man. He had never wronged me. He had never given me insult. For his gold I had no desire. I think it was his eye! Yes, it was this! He had the eye of a vulture – a pale blue eye, with a film over it. Whenever it fell upon me, my blood ran cold; and so by degrees – very gradually – I made up my mind to take the life of the old man, and thus rid myself of the eye forever.*
>
> Edgar Allan Poe, 'The Tell-Tale Heart'

❻ On a separate piece of paper, write a **paragraph** of **first-person narrative** that reveals character, like this one. If you wish, use the same opening: *'It is impossible to say ...'*. Make your character one of the following:

- An eccentric inventor
- Someone who collects something unusual
- A fan who thinks of a way to get closer to someone they admire

TEST YOUR UNDERSTANDING

❼ Write the **beginning of a story** that focuses on a **character with a difficult choice to make**. It could be in the **third person** (he/she) or the **first person** (I). Include:

- A description of their appearance
- Revealing action
- Revealing dialogue
- Something to show the character's motivation

....

....

....

....

....

....

....

....

....

....

....

....

PROGRESS LOG [tick the correct box]   Needs more work ▪   Getting there ▪   Under control ▪

Writing to describe

EXAM BASICS

What you have to do:

- When writing a description, it is vital to come up with some imaginative ideas and engage your reader through interesting use of structure.

Remember:

- Structure your description to draw the reader in and lead them through it.
- Use language to make your description come to life.

PRACTISE YOUR SKILLS

GENERATING IDEAS

❶ Write a chain of at least **five word associations** (any linked words that come into your head) that develop from the given word. See a) as an example.

a) baker	*bread*	*loaf*	*slice*	*knife*	*cut*	*blood*
b) cloud	....	....	....	....	....	....
c) train	....	....	....	....	....	....
d) rocket	....	....	....	....	....	....
e) tiger	....	....	....	....	....	....

❷ Compose an **interesting descriptive opening** by adding a **vivid or powerful word or phrase** in the blanks below:

a) *A(n)* [adjective] .... *cloud* [present-tense verb] ....
across the sky like a [noun phrase] ....

b) [adverb] .... , *the* [adjective] ....
train chugged through the [adjective] .... *valley like a*
[noun phrase] ....

❸ Now write similar **opening sentences** using each of the other **nouns** from the word chains listed in Task 1:

a) **rocket** ....

....

....

b) **tiger** ....

....

....

❹ Rewrite the sentences below adding **descriptive words and details**. Try to suggest a different **feeling** for each sentence.

a) *The balloon drifted above the field of cows.* ....

....

....

b) *A cloud of bluebells fills the wood.* ....

....

....

STRUCTURING YOUR DESCRIPTION

In the following description of a room, an overview gradually focuses in on a significant detail.

> The room has hardly changed since I last saw it, so many years ago, though a faint odour of dampness hangs on the air, and the floral patterns of the wallpaper and three-piece suite seem duller than I remember them, the sofa cushions a little more tired and saggy, like old balloons a week after a party.
>
> Beside the bay window is the upright piano, still a gleaming chestnut, a faded book of sheet music open, waiting to be played on tinkling, slightly cronky keys. On top, a willow-pattern Chinese vase, with dry grasses, a carved wooden giraffe. And in between them, gazing at me across the years, a framed photo: a handsome, hopeful man in wartime uniform, looking down lovingly at the bride beside him, who smiles right into the camera.

❺ Write an **imaginative description** of a different **room or place** which, like this one, moves from the **general to a particular detail**. You could include:

- Hints of the first-person speaker's relationship to the room, as in the phrase 'so many years ago'
- A simile, as in 'like old balloons a week after a party'
- An appeal to one or more senses, as in 'faint odour of dampness' and 'tinkling, slightly cronky keys'

....

....

....

....

....

....

....

....

....

....

6 Now, on a separate piece of paper, write a **plan** for an **imaginative description** using a structure that moves across a scene **from near to far**. For example, you could follow this structure to write a description of a beach:

Very close	A beach ball rolling past and bouncing off a nearby sandcastle
Nearby	Four people playing volleyball
Medium distance	People paddling and wading into the sea
Far away	A distant fisherman, surf crashing on the rocks across the bay

TEST YOUR UNDERSTANDING

7 Write a **description** of either a **favourite room** or a **derelict factory**.
- Begin by generating **ideas**, using the **word association technique** in Task 1.
- Using one of the **structures** given in Tasks 5 and 6, plan what you will **describe** in each paragraph.
- Write an effective **opening sentence** (see Tasks 2 and 3).
- Use interesting **descriptive language and details** to create the feeling you want your readers to have when they read your description (see Task 4).

....
....
....
....
....
....
....
....
....
....
....
....
....
....
....

PROGRESS LOG [tick the correct box]   Needs more work ■   Getting there ■   Under control ■

Writing to narrate

A05 A06
PAPER 1,
SECTION B, Q5

EXAM BASICS

What you have to do:

- Whether you are writing a story based on a picture or a written prompt, you need to plan your narrative, choose a viewpoint and structure your ideas effectively.

Remember:

- Explore ideas suggested by the picture or prompt, and then choose one.
- Structure the way in which you reveal and withhold information.
- Write an attention-grabbing opening, and end with a sense of resolution.

PRACTISE YOUR SKILLS

GENERATING IDEAS AND PLANNING

❶ Imagine you are given this exam prompt:

Write a story in which a disappointment leads to a surprisingly positive outcome.

Use the space below to **generate ideas** for what you might write about. One idea has been added already.

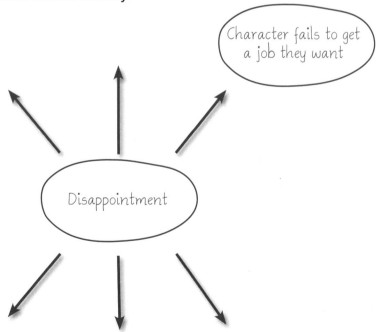

CREATING A PLOT

❷ Using your ideas from Task 1, fill out the planning table below, which
    gives an example plan.

Plot stage	Example	Your plan
1. Trigger – setting off action	Errol is in dead-end job and sees his dream job advertised.	
2. Successes and reverses	He applies, gets an interview and thinks he's got the job. A letter arrives – he's failed.	
3. Crisis	Errol has already handed in his notice and gets into debt.	
4. Climax	He can't pay his rent. His landlord confronts him, and threatens him with eviction.	
5. Resolution	Errol takes up busking, is discovered and becomes star.	

CHOOSING A VIEWPOINT AND TENSE

❸ Rewrite the following **third-person** story extract in the **first person**.

> Errol hadn't touched his guitar for years, and it felt strange in his hands. Tentatively, he
> tried a chord of C, and was surprised to discover the instrument was almost in tune. He
> tweaked up the D-string a semitone and tried again: perfect.

....

....

....

....

❹ Underline the **verbs** in this **past-tense** story extract and write them in the
    present tense above the original verb.

> Davina wriggled down the passage, the light from her head torch pooling just in front of
> her. Was it getting tighter, or was she just panicking?
>
> 'Come on,' said Molly. 'You can do it!'
>
> 'I can't,' she sobbed. 'I'm going back.' But this was easier said than done. She struggled to
> hook her feet in the rock and pull back, but she was jammed tight.

REORDERING TIME: FLASHBACKS

5 Write a **flashback** to the story extract in Task 4, in which we see what led up to the events described. You could begin, '*The previous day, when Molly had asked her if …*'.

....

....

....

....

TEST YOUR UNDERSTANDING

6 Imagine you have been given this exam prompt:

Write a story in which someone is rescued from a dangerous situation.

Plan the story. You will have to decide:

- What is the **danger**, and how does the character get into it?
- How are they **rescued**?
- How does the **main character respond** to the situation?
- Is **anyone else** with them, and what is their involvement?
- What **tense** and **person** (first or third) will you use?
- Will you use a **flashback** (e.g. 'Earlier that day …')?

....

....

....

....

....

....

....

....

....

....

....

....

....

PROGRESS LOG [tick the correct box]   Needs more work ■   Getting there ■   Under control ■

CHAPTER 4: Paper 2, Section A: Reading non-fiction texts

Deciding what is true or false

A01

PAPER 2,
SECTION A, Q1

EXAM BASICS

What you have to do:

- Identify four true statements out of a list of eight.

Remember:

- Focus on the section of the source indicated in the exam paper.
- Only select four statements.

PRACTISE YOUR SKILLS

Source A. Read this extract from a modern non-fiction article which expresses a viewpoint on landscape and the environment.

Can you put a price on the beauty of the natural world?

George Monbiot, *The Guardian*, 22 April 2014 (theguardian.com)

George Orwell warned that 'the logical end of mechanical progress is to reduce the human being to something resembling a brain in a bottle'. This is a story of how it happens.

On the outskirts of Sheffield there is a wood which, some 800 years ago, was used by the monks of Kirkstead Abbey to produce charcoal for smelting iron. For local people, Smithy Wood is freighted with stories. Among the trees you can imagine your way into another world. The application to plant a motorway service station in the middle of it, wiping out half the wood and fragmenting the rest, might have been unthinkable a few months ago. No longer.

When the environment secretary, Owen Paterson, first began talking about biodiversity offsetting – replacing habitats you trash with new ones created elsewhere – his officials made it clear that it would not apply to ancient woodland. But in January Paterson said he was prepared to drop this restriction as long as more trees were planted than destroyed.

His officials quickly explained that such a trade-off would be 'highly unlikely' and was 'very hypothetical'. But the company that wants to build the service station wasn't slow to see the possibilities. It is offering to replace Smithy Wood with '60,000 trees [...] planted on 16 hectares of local land close to the site'. Who cares whether a tree is a hunched and fissured coppiced oak, worked by people for centuries, or a sapling[1] planted beside a slip-road with a rabbit guard around it?

As Ronald Reagan remarked, when contemplating the destruction of California's giant redwoods, 'a tree is a tree'. Who, for that matter, would care if the old masters in the National Gallery were replaced by the prints being sold in its shop? In swapping our ancient places for generic clusters of chainstores and generic lines of saplings, the offsetters would also destroy our stories. [...]

But this is the way it's going now: everything will be fungible,[2] nothing will be valued for its own sake, place and past and love and enchantment will have no meaning. The natural world will be reduced to a column of figures.

sapling[1] – newly planted young tree

fungible[2] – replaceable by something supposedly identical

GETTING THE FACTS STRAIGHT

❶ Answer these **factual questions** about the article:

a) What did George Orwell warn?

....

....

b) What was Smithy Wood formerly used for?

....

....

c) What is 'biodiversity offsetting'?

....

....

d) Where does the company want to build a service station?

....

e) How does the company intend to make up for cutting down trees?

....

❷ Based on the first two paragraphs of the article, choose **four true**
   statements below. Tick the boxes of the ones that you think are true.

   a) Orwell feared that mechanical progress could be
      dehumanising. ☐

   b) Monbiot is in favour of all mechanical progress. ☐

   c) Some monks made iron 800 years ago. ☐

   d) Smithy Wood contains a portal into another world. ☐

   e) Monbiot thinks that it has become easier to destroy
      woodland. ☐

   f) Local people are frightened to go into Smithy Wood. ☐

   g) Iron is used for making charcoal. ☐

   h) Local people tell stories about Smithy Wood. ☐

❸ Based on paragraphs 3 and 4 of the article, choose **four** statements
   below which are **true**. Tick the boxes of the ones that you
   think are true.

   a) Owen Paterson is opposed to tree-planting. ☐

   b) George Monbiot is opposed to biodiversity offsetting. ☐

   c) Monbiot is concerned about rabbits eating the trees. ☐

   d) Monbiot says that ancient woodland was once protected
      from biodiversity offsetting. ☐

   e) Biodiversity offsetting rules have been relaxed. ☐

   f) The company wants to plant new trees near Smithy Wood. ☐

   g) Monbiot does not care about the age of trees, so long as
      new ones are planted. ☐

   h) Officials have agreed to the company's proposals. ☐

TEST YOUR UNDERSTANDING

❹ Which **two** true statements in Task 3 are **implied** rather than made
   explicit? Why?

....

....

....

....

....

....

....

....

PROGRESS LOG [tick the correct box]   Needs more work ☐   Getting there ☐   Under control ☐

Summarising texts

EXAM BASICS

What you have to do:

- Write a summary of the similarities and differences between the content of two sources.
- Infer implicit meaning and combine information from both sources.

Remember:

- Focus on whatever aspect of the sources is identified in the question.
- Write full sentences, not notes.

PRACTISE YOUR SKILLS

Source B. Read this nineteenth-century letter to *The Times* and then tackle the tasks that follow.

---

24 February 1898

To the Editor of The Times.

Sir, As the Great Western Railway Company's (New Works) Bill, will shortly come on for second reading in the House of Commons, I should like to call public attention to the disastrous effect which such a railway would have upon Thames scenery.

There will be three bridges (presumably of the usual lattice girder type) across the river, with the necessary viaducts and embankments on the low meadows on either side; there will also be a high embankment in the Henley Valley, crossing the corner of the Lion Meadow, with a bridge over the Oxford–London road at the foot of White Hill.

I need hardly point out that works of this character will not only completely spoil many of the views of the wooded hills, but the charm of Henley will [also] be destroyed.

Thus the enjoyment of the public while in pursuit of healthy pleasure will be seriously interfered with, and those using the Thames – the Queen's highway – who now appreciate the natural beauties of the river will have their pleasure diminished; and the name of one more place will have to be removed from the list of sights that can only be seen in England.

The feeling of the 'rowing world' is unanimous against the scheme; the Henley Regatta Committee, the Oxford University Boat Club, the Cambridge University Boat Club, and the Leander Club have all passed resolutions condemning the proposed railway; and many other clubs have concurred therein. May I, therefore, venture to ask your all-powerful aid in giving publicity to the matter, in the hope that on the second reading of the Bill an undertaking may be obtained for the withdrawal from the Bill of this objectionable railway?

> *It is difficult to imagine the reasons that have induced the company to put forward such a scheme, unless it be for the purpose of keeping the district free from competition by some other railway company. It can hardly be alleged seriously that it is required for local traffic, while the town of Henley and the local landowners are petitioning against the Bill.*
> *I am, Sir, your obedient servant,*
>
> HERBERT THOMAS STEWARD, *Chairman of the Committee of Management of Henley Royal Regatta, Henley-on-Thames*

LISTING VIEWS AND ATTITUDES

❶ Explain in your own words the **basic view** Steward is expressing in this sentence:

I should like to call public attention to the disastrous effect which such a railway would have upon Thames scenery.

You could start: *In Steward's view the railway would* ....

....

....

....

....

❷ Fill in the gaps in the sentence below, which summarises the **view** Steward is presenting in his **second paragraph**:

There will be huge .... to the landscape in the .... of the

railway, because of the structures that will be .... to support it.

❸ What **evidence** is there that local people do not want the railway?

....

....

....

❹ In your own words, **list** the other points made by Steward **supporting his appeal** in his letter.

....

....

....

....

....

❺ Now remind yourself of **Source A**, the Monbiot article (on pages 38–9). **Summarise** in one sentence the **main point** Monbiot makes in his article.

....

....

....

⑥ Use the table below to make notes on the **similarities** and **differences** between the views of the two sources. (Jot down any suitable **quotations**.)

Consider:

- What each writer **objects** to
- Their **reasons** for objecting
- **How hopeful** they appear to be
- What **evidence** you find for their views

Source A	Source B

TEST YOUR UNDERSTANDING

❼ Use your table to write one or more paragraphs **summarising** the similarities and differences between the views in **Source A** (Monbiot) and **Source B** (Steward).

Remember:

- Write in **sentences**.
- Provide **evidence**.

....

....

....

....

....

....

....

....

....

....

....

....

....

....

....

....

....

....

....

....

....

....

....

....

....

PROGRESS LOG [tick the correct box]   Needs more work ☐   Getting there ☐   Under control ☐

Understanding persuasive language

A02

PAPER 2,
SECTION A, Q3

PRACTISE YOUR SKILLS

REGISTER AND TONE

❶ Reread **Source A** (George Monbiot, pages 38–9), paragraph 2. Which of the words listed below might you use for the **tone** in which Monbiot describes:

a) Smithy Wood?

....

b) The plan to build a service station?

....

....

(You might find that more than one word fits in each case.)

> angry   positive   respectful   humorous
>
> incredulous (disbelieving)   appreciative   puzzled   shocked
>
> critical   dismissive   sad   annoyed   indignant

❷ Reread **Source B** (Steward), paragraph 4 ('Thus the enjoyment …'). Which of the words in the list above could be used to describe its **tone**?

....

....

❸ The tone of **Source B** changes slightly in paragraph 5, where the writer lists groups opposing the railway. Write a **sentence** describing the **tone** and explaining what produces it. You could start:

The tone becomes more ....

....

....

TION TEXTS

AL DEVICES

 TO DO

the table below.

Device	Definition	Example
Tricolon (triple, triad)		... the accusation is groundless, dishonest, and libellous.
	Question making a point rather than seeking an answer	Is that the best they can offer?
Alliteration		This is cold comfort at best.
Parallelism	*Achieving contrast by repeating a grammatical form*	They claim that space exploration offers hope and inspiration; actually it ... **[complete the sentence]**
Simile	*Image comparing two things using 'like', 'as' or 'than'*	
Metaphor		Samuel ploughed through his homework. (He does not literally 'plough' his homework.)
	Giving human or godlike qualities to something abstract	Our patriotism is sleeping for now, but soon it will awake!
Juxtaposition	*Presenting two contrasting things close together for effect*	I exchanged my luxury en suite apartment for a [complete the sentence]

❺ The whole of paragraph 4 in **Source B** ('Thus the enjoyment ...') forms a **rhetorical device**.

   a) What is the **device**? ....

   b) What is its **effect**? ....

   ....

❻ What **rhetorical devices** are used in the following phrases in **Source A**, and what is the **effect** of each?

   a) 'brain in a bottle' ....

   ....

   b) 'freighted with stories' (Hint: 'freight' trains carry goods.) ....

   ....

   c) 'generic clusters of chainstores and generic lines of saplings'...

   ....

EMOTIVE LANGUAGE

❼ Both Monbiot and Steward use emotive language to communicate their viewpoint. Explain the **effect** of the following words and phrases:

a) 'wiping out half the wood' (Source A)

....

....

b) 'habitats you trash' (Source A)

....

....

c) 'The natural world will be reduced to a column of figures' (Source A)

....

....

d) 'disastrous' (Source B)

....

....

e) 'pursuit of healthy pleasure' (Source B)

....

....

f) 'natural beauties' (Source B)

....

....

TEST YOUR UNDERSTANDING

❽ Choose either **Source A** (pages 38–9) or **Source B** (pages 41–2) and write a paragraph explaining which **three persuasive techniques** in the source you find the most **effective**, and **why**. Continue on a separate piece of paper if necessary.

....

....

....

....

....

....

....

....

....

....

PROGRESS LOG [tick the correct box]   Needs more work ■   Getting there ■   Under control ■

Comparing viewpoints and techniques

PAPER 2,
SECTION A, Q4

EXAM BASICS

What you have to do:

- Compare the whole of two sources.
- Compare how the two authors convey their viewpoints.

Remember:

- Focus on the writers' techniques.
- Include references to details and the overall structure.
- Provide textual evidence.

PRACTISE YOUR SKILLS

IDENTIFYING ATTITUDES AND TECHNIQUES

Read these two paragraphs, then answer the questions.

Paragraph A

Every insignificant little place has its festival these days. There are street festivals, festivals in village halls, festivals in the woods, and festivals by rivers. People seem intent on partying like there's no tomorrow. Perhaps it's a symptom of a nation swimming in Lottery funding and no one knowing quite what to do with it. Perhaps it's all about local wannabes, big fish in small ponds, competing with each other to be Most Important Person in their community. Or perhaps they're all trying to take their minds off the imminent collapse of society as we know it. At any rate, every time I see a festival I want to run a mile.

Paragraph B

The Little Buglip Festival is under way, and I'm lapping it up. The sun is smiling on a quintessential English field – the kind that farmers have tilled for centuries, and where cows were lazily grazing only yesterday. Children run about with butterflies on sticks, teenage girls serve real lemonade beneath striped awnings, and a clown on stilts staggering like a daddy-long-legs is announcing that the local choir is about to perform. What's not to like? And this is just one of half a dozen similar events in the area this summer. Community spirit is alive and well in the British countryside.

---

❶ Write a **sentence** comparing the **attitudes** of the two writers
to festivals. Start:

Author A's view of village festivals is ....

....

....

....

....

Answer the following tasks on a separate piece of paper.

❷ Looking at Paragraph A:
   a) How does the **opening sentence** signal a **dismissive attitude**?
   b) What is the **effect of repetition** in the second sentence?
   c) What type of **image** is 'swimming in Lottery funding', and what does it **imply**?
   d) How does the sentence beginning 'Perhaps it's all about …' convey a **negative view**?
   e) What is the **effect** of the final sentence?

❸ Looking at Paragraph B:
   a) How does the **opening sentence** signal an **enthusiastic attitude**?
   b) **Where** and **how** does the writer show **appreciation for tradition**?
   c) What **rhetorical device** is used in the sentence beginning 'Children run …', and what it its **effect**?
   d) What **simile** is used, and what is its **effect**?
   e) What is the **effect** of the **final sentence**?

FINDING EVIDENCE

❹ Find **evidence** that:
   a) Paragraph A's writer is **pessimistic** about society
   b) Paragraph B's writer is **positive** about rural life

❺ Returning to **Source A** (Monbiot, pages 38–9) and **Source B** (Steward, pages 41–2), find **evidence** that:
   a) Both writers try to give themselves some form of **personal authority** (Monbiot in paragraphs 1–3, Steward in paragraphs 2 and 5)
   b) Steward thinks that the **sense of his argument** is **self-evident** (paragraph 3 and opening to paragraph 5)
   c) Monbiot thinks that the need to preserve ancient woodland should **still** be **self-evident** (end of paragraph 2)
   d) Both writers want to **preserve natural beauty**
   e) Monbiot is **angrier** than Steward
   f) Steward is **more hopeful** than Monbiot

STRUCTURE

❻ In which paragraphs do (a) Monbiot and (b) Steward **explain the problem** as they see it?

❼ In which paragraphs do (a) Monbiot and (b) Steward **put forward their key arguments**?

❽ How does each writer (Monbiot and Steward) **conclude**?

TEST YOUR UNDERSTANDING

9 Look back over your answers in this unit. Then write a **comparison** of **Source A** (Monbiot) and **Source B** (Steward). Focus on their:

- **Views**
- **Methods**

Remember to provide **evidence** from both texts.

....
....
....
....
....
....
....
....
....
....
....
....
....
....
....
....
....
....
....
....
....
....
....
....
....
....

PROGRESS LOG [tick the correct box]   Needs more work ■   Getting there ■   Under control ■

CHAPTER 5: Paper 2, Section B: Writing to present a viewpoint

Key conventions of persuasive texts

A05 A06

PAPER 2,
SECTION B, Q5

EXAM BASICS

In Paper 2, Section B, you will be asked to express your views on an issue related to the theme of the Section A sources.

Remember:

- Write for the purpose, audience and form stated in the question.
- Use persuasive language, organised for maximum impact.
- Write in fairly formal standard English, and aim for accurate spelling, punctuation and grammar.

PRACTISE YOUR SKILLS

RHETORICAL DEVICES

❶ Using the examples of **rhetorical devices as models**, write your own. If you need to, use the first few words of the example provided.

Device	Example	Your example
Tricolon (triple, triad)	*These views are ignorant, prejudiced and dangerous.*	These views are …
Rhetorical question	*Have we forgotten the meaning of justice?*	Have we forgotten …
Alliteration	*Our town is plagued by teenage tearaways.*	Our town/city/village is …
Parallelism	*Supporters call hunting a necessary and traditional sport. We call it an unnecessary and barbaric abomination.*	Supporters call …
Listing	*I have addressed audiences in London, Liverpool, Newcastle, Cardiff and Bristol …*	I have …
Repetition	*The EU has championed the environment, the EU has championed fair trade, the EU has …*	The … has …
Irony	*A nuclear accident would be rather inconvenient.*	A … would …

❷ Consider the following question:

'Lowering the voting age to 16 would be fair to teenagers and benefit society as a whole.'

Write a letter to the House of Commons expressing your views on this statement.

On a separate piece of paper, write **one** paragraph **agreeing or disagreeing**. Try to use four **rhetorical devices**, in any order. Add other sentences in between if you wish.

PROVIDING EVIDENCE

❸ Complete the sentences below in response to the question in Task 2. Follow the specific instructions for each.

a) Provide **anecdotal evidence** – in the form of a short informal story to support your argument:
   The other day I was listening to three teenagers …

   ....

   ....

b) Present a **statistic** to justify your views:
   A staggering 87 per cent of teenagers …

   ....

   ....

c) Present evidence by **quoting a study**:
   A recent study carried out by the University of Birmingham found that …

   ....

   ....

DIRECT APPEALS AND CALLS TO ACTION

❹ On a separate piece of paper, rewrite this sample exam response from the point of view of a student. Make it more effective by using some or all of the **pronouns** 'I', 'you', 'we', 'me', 'us' and the **possessives** 'my', 'your', 'our', and by **addressing the reader** or listener in a simple, direct manner (e.g. 'Look at how …')

It is often possible to hear teenagers discussing political issues, even though they may not identify them as such. For example, the cost of school uniform is, in the view of some people, a political issue.

People see graffiti scrawled on underpass walls and they assume this is just pointless vandalism. But it could be considered as a demand for a voice in society. Students should ask their MPs to consider them as near-adults, who will become the future of this society. Society as a whole needs to see them as such, before they come to regard politics as boring and irrelevant.

❺ Fill in the blanks to form **calls to action**:

Every £5 you donate will help to preserve a ....

for orphaned .... *like* ....

Every .... *deserves a* ....

Give generously now, before it's ....

TEST YOUR UNDERSTANDING

❻ Write an **opening paragraph** in response to the following task:

'Time spent on social media is time wasted.'

*Write an article for a youth-market magazine **expressing your views** on this statement.*

Use:

- Some well-chosen **rhetorical devices**
- **Evidence** – which you can make up if necessary
- **Direct appeal** and/or a **call to action**

....

....

....

....

....

....

....

....

....

....

....

....

....

....

....

....

....

....

....

....

....

....

PROGRESS LOG [tick the correct box]   Needs more work ☐   Getting there ☐   Under control ☐

Using persuasive language

PAPER 2,
SECTION B, Q5

EXAM BASICS

It is important that your written answer presents a clear viewpoint, and communicates using an appropriate tone and style.

Remember:

● Adapt your tone and style to meet your audience's needs.

● Communicate imaginatively using appropriate persuasive language.

PRACTISE YOUR SKILLS

TONE AND REGISTER

❶ Draw a line to match each example of **tone/register** to the **form/audience** from this task about disabled facilities.

Form/audience

a) Article for broadsheet newspaper

b) Letter to headteacher

c) Speech to teenagers of similar age

Example of tone/register

'Are you up for changing things? Of course you are. Protest to the Head, get out there and put up posters, make some noise on the web – whatever it takes!'

'You have a duty to make sure that every child in the school can learn in a supportive manner, regardless of where they've come from, or their needs or abilities. Isn't it true that the school is falling some way short of where it should be?'

'We can no longer allow schools to exist as locations where discrimination continues. It is our duty to influence the authorities, mobilise on the streets, utilise social media and do whatever is required.'

EMOTIVE LANGUAGE – INCREASING THE IMPACT

❷ Read this paragraph from a speech to local councillors.

> I am a <u>little bit angry</u> about the <u>rather bad</u> state of facilities for the disabled. It is <u>not really OK</u> that we have allowed this <u>bad</u> situation to arise. I <u>really do ask you</u> to consider how things can be improved for everyone concerned. It would be <u>quite good</u> if all schools were properly resourced by the end of the year.

Replace the **underlined words and phrases** with more **powerful alternatives**. For example, where could 'furious' be used?

❸ Use the idea of creating an **image, anecdote** or **'mini'-story** to begin a speech about the lack of disabled facilities in schools across a city. Start:

Picture this: a little girl in a wheelchair ....

....

....

SENTENCES FOR EFFECT

❹ Read this extract from an article about the price of tickets to Premier League football games.

> *I got a terrible shock the other day when I tried to buy a ticket for a top football game at the weekend. The price of the ticket was £55, which I thought was ridiculous. For that I could spend a night in a B & B. I could buy a posh meal out for two people, including drinks. I could buy a fitness watch or a designer pair of glasses. They must be joking charging that amount, I thought.*

Rewrite this paragraph so it has more **impact** by creating some **minor, short** and some **longer sentences**. You can take out or add words as needed. For example, you could start:

What a shock! ....

....

....

....

....

....

IMAGERY

Read this example of a **persuasive sentence** from an article.

> *The almost imperceptible change in our high streets as betting shops appear is like a virus slowly worming its way around the body, damaging the organs one by one.*

❺ Underline the **simile** used here.

❻ Now, complete these two sentences using further **similes**.

Each betting shop draws customers in, rather like the way ....

....

....

Once someone is bitten by the betting bug, it is like ....

....

....

TEST YOUR UNDERSTANDING

❼ Read this task:

'*Printed books are history. The sooner all libraries, whether in our schools or in our town, are closed, the better.*'

Write an article for a local newspaper in which you explain your point of view on this statement.

Write at least **two paragraphs** from the article. Make sure you:

- Use **powerful and/or emotive language** and **imagery** as appropriate.
- Use an **appropriate tone/register** for the audience.
- **Vary sentence type** for effect.

Planning and structure

A05 A06
PAPER 2,
SECTION B, Q5

EXAM BASICS

When responding to Paper 2, Section B, make sure that you plan your writing carefully, structuring it for maximum persuasive impact.

Remember:

- Use paragraphs – perhaps with one key idea in each one.
- Organise your ideas logically.
- Use connectives to link up your ideas.

PRACTISE YOUR SKILLS

PLANNING

❶ Consider this task:

'Space exploration is a waste of time and resources that could solve problems here on earth.'

Write the text of a speech for a debate at your school or college in which you explain your views on this statement.

Choose your point of view.

Fill in the table below to **plan a response**:

Paragraph	What you need	Possible ideas
1	Compelling introduction, including, e.g. a quotation or statistic	e.g. 'One small leap for man; one giant leap for mankind'
2	Why, in your view, exploration takes place, e.g. thirst for knowledge	
3	Benefits of exploration	
4	More benefits?	
5	Arguments against, and what you think of them	
6	Weighing up and conclusion	

❷ Consider this task:

'People spend too much time and money on pets. The world would be a better place if pets were banned.'

Write an article for an animal lovers' magazine arguing for or against this view.

Read through this extended plan for a response to the task. Then organise the points into a **logical sequence** by writing the numbers 1 to 9 in the boxes.

a) Pets released into wild unbalance ecosystem (e.g. fish) ☐

b) Cats calm people down and provide company ☐

c) Half the world lives on less than £2 a day (many people spend more per day on a pet). Money spent on pets could end world poverty ☐

d) However, these benefits are heavily outweighed by the problems, so I agree with this statement ☐

e) Dogs bite people (e.g. postal workers) ☐

f) Cats destroying bird life, voles, etc. ☐

g) Dogs keep people fit – walks ☐

h) Popularity of pets. 'Man's best friend'. 40% of UK households have a pet; 24% have dogs, 17% cats. Cost of keeping dogs and cats ☐

i) Dog fouling – disgusting and disease-carrying ☐

TOPIC SENTENCES

❸ On a separate piece of paper, write **topic sentences** to introduce each of the points in the plan for Task 2, except for the first and last.

Hint: A topic sentence for Point c) might read, 'Pets are a luxury the world cannot afford.'

CONNECTIVES

❹ Add **connectives** to the following extract to make the ideas **flow** smoothly. Choose from the connectives below the extract.

Human beings have evolved through their natural curiosity. ....
..............................., it might be said that in the case of space exploration this is 'idle' curiosity. We really have no need to know what conditions are like on Mars. ...., even getting an unmanned craft there is hugely expensive, ... there is a strong chance that it will not even be able to land, ...
.... the money will have been wasted.

> moreover   in which case   added to which   yet
> nevertheless   however   despite this

5 On a separate piece of paper, rewrite the following student response, making it more effective by adding **connectives**. They can go at the start of paragraphs or sentences, or mid-sentence, as in 'Dogs, *for example*, require …'. Make any necessary changes to **punctuation**.

Some people think that money spent on pets is extravagant. It would be better spent on solving world poverty. They claim that dogs are a public nuisance, that cats kill wild birds. I think that pets are well worth the money they cost. They bring such great benefits to their human owners. I think the negatives of pet ownership are exaggerated.

TEST YOUR UNDERSTANDING

6 Read this task:

'Teenagers nowadays have far easier lives than their parents or grandparents did in their teens.'

Write an article for a broadsheet newspaper's weekend magazine expressing your views on this statement.

Write a brief plan using the space provided, then write the **first two paragraphs** of the response. Begin the first with an **attention-grabbing feature**, and the second with a **topic sentence**. Include at least **two connectives**. You may need to use additional sheets of paper.

PROGRESS LOG [tick the correct box] Needs more work ☐ Getting there ☐ Under control ☐

CHAPTER 6: GCSE English Language practice paper

Paper 1: Explorations in creative reading and writing

Time allowed: 1 hour 45 minutes
Complete this practice paper in your own notebook or on separate sheets of paper

SOURCE A

The Jungle Book, by Rudyard Kipling

Mowgli is a boy who is able to speak to animals. Akela is a wolf, and Rama the head bull of the buffalo herd. In this extract, Mowgli enacts a plan to catch the tiger, Shere Khan.

Mowgli's plan was simple enough. All he wanted to do was to make a big circle uphill and get at the head of the ravine, and then take the bulls down it and catch Shere Khan between the bulls and the cows; for he knew that after a meal and a full drink Shere Khan would not be in
5 any condition to fight or to clamber up the sides of the ravine. He was soothing the buffaloes now by voice, and Akela had dropped far to the rear, only whimpering once or twice to hurry the rear-guard. It was a long, long circle, for they did not wish to get too near the ravine and give Shere Khan warning. At last Mowgli rounded up the bewildered
10 herd at the head of the ravine on a grassy patch that sloped steeply down to the ravine itself. From that height you could see across the tops of the trees down to the plain below; but what Mowgli looked at was the sides of the ravine, and he saw with a great deal of satisfaction that they ran nearly straight up and down, while the vines and creepers
15 that hung over them would give no foothold to a tiger who wanted to get out.

'Let them breathe, Akela,' he said, holding up his hand. 'They have not winded him yet. Let them breathe. I must tell Shere Khan who comes. We have him in the trap.'
20 He put his hands to his mouth and shouted down the ravine – it was almost like shouting down a tunnel – and the echoes jumped from rock to rock.

After a long time there came back the drawling, sleepy snarl of a full-fed tiger just wakened.
25 'Who calls?' said Shere Khan, and a splendid peacock fluttered up out of the ravine screeching.

'I, Mowgli. Cattle thief, it is time to come to the Council Rock! Down – hurry them down, Akela! Down, Rama, down!'

30   The herd paused for an instant at the edge of the slope, but Akela gave tongue in the full hunting-yell, and they pitched over one after the other, just as steamers shoot rapids, the sand and stones spurting up round them. Once started, there was no chance of stopping, and before they were fairly in the bed of the ravine Rama winded Shere Khan and bellowed.

35   'Ha! Ha!' said Mowgli, on his back. 'Now thou knowest!' and the torrent of black horns, foaming muzzles, and staring eyes whirled down the ravine just as boulders go down in floodtime; the weaker buffaloes being shouldered out to the sides of the ravine where they tore through the creepers. They knew what the business was before

40   them – the terrible charge of the buffalo herd against which no tiger can hope to stand. Shere Khan heard the thunder of their hoofs, picked himself up, and lumbered down the ravine, looking from side to side for some way of escape, but the walls of the ravine were straight and he had to hold on, heavy with his dinner and his drink, willing to do

45   anything rather than fight. The herd splashed through the pool he had just left, bellowing till the narrow cut[1] rang. Mowgli heard an answering bellow from the foot of the ravine, saw Shere Khan turn (the tiger knew if the worst came to the worst it was better to meet the bulls than the cows with their calves), and then Rama tripped,

50   stumbled, and went on again over something soft, and, with the bulls at his heels, crashed full into the other herd, while the weaker buffaloes were lifted clean off their feet by the shock of the meeting. That charge carried both herds out into the plain, goring and stamping and snorting. Mowgli watched his time, and slipped off Rama's neck,

55   laying about him right and left with his stick.

    'Quick, Akela! Break them up. Scatter them, or they will be fighting one another. Drive them away, Akela. Hai, Rama! Hai, hai, hai! my children. Softly now, softly! It is all over.'

[1]*cut* – ravine

Section A: Reading

Answer **all** questions in this section.

You are advised to spend about 45 minutes on this section.

❶ Read again the first part of the source, **lines 1–15**.

List **four** things from this part of the source about Mowgli's plan and its chances of working.

[4 marks]

❷ Look in detail at **lines 16–32**.

How does the writer use language here to create a sense of drama and anticipation?

You could include the writer's choice of:

- words and phrases
- language features and techniques
- sentence forms.

[8 marks]

❸ You now need to think about the **whole** of the **source**.

How has the writer structured the text to interest you as a reader?

You could write about:

- what the writer focuses your attention on at the beginning
- how and why the writer changes this focus as the source develops
- any other structural features that interest you.

[8 marks]

❹ Focus this part of your answer on the last part of the source from **line 33 to the end**.

A reviewer wrote: 'This part of the extract where the buffaloes stampede into the ravine is highly effective in bringing the episode to a tense and exciting climax.'

To what extent do you agree?

In your response, you could:

- consider your own impressions of how the mood is created
- evaluate how the writer creates a sense of excitement and action
- support your response with references to the text.

[20 marks]

Section B: Writing

You are advised to spend about 45 minutes on this section.

Write in full sentences.

You are reminded of the need to plan your answer.

You should leave enough time to check your work at the end.

❺ You have been invited to produce a piece of creative writing about some form of hunt.

Either: Write a story involving one or more fierce animals as suggested by this picture:

Or: Write a story in which someone plans and springs a trap on an enemy.

(24 marks for content and organisation

16 marks for technical accuracy)

[40 marks]

Paper 2: Writers' viewpoints and perspectives

Time allowed: 1 hour 45 minutes
Complete this practice paper in your own notebook or on separate sheets of paper

SOURCE A

The old debate: punish prisoners, or rehabilitate them?

Eleanor Muffitt, *Daily Telegraph*, **18 December 2013**

Debates over how to treat prisoners have gone on since imprisonment began: should the prison system leave inmates to fester in cold cells, with punishment and deterrence as the goal of incarceration? Or should it let them wander from classroom to games room, preaching rehabilitation into society as its main aim?

5   Alan Weston, currently serving his second rape sentence at HMP Frankland, complained to prison newspaper *Inside Time* this month saying he couldn't access National Prison Radio (NPR) on his new digital system. Mr Weston's complaint raises the age-old question – should we give criminals the same basic luxuries we take for granted, or would that be spoiling them?

10   Although the UK spends a higher amount of GDP on public order than the US or any EU countries, our jails are highly ineffective. With over 83,000 prisoners currently locked away, England and Wales have a staggering imprisonment rate of 150 per 100,000 of the population. Our prisons have been officially overcrowded since 1994; nearly 14,000 current inmates are serving indeterminate
15   sentences.

If lowering the number of criminals is the reason behind imprisonment, recent figures point to a failing system: almost three quarters of under-18s are reconvicted within a year of release. As James Bell, an American lawyer and prison reform activist, said: 'As it stands now, justice systems are extremely
20   expensive, do not rehabilitate, but in fact make the people that experience them worse.'

In response to worldwide alarm over the ineffectiveness of how we manage criminals, a growing number of prisons are embracing a new style of incarceration. By giving inmates more responsibility, comfort, and freedom
25   within the prison walls, governors say they are offering prisoners the chance to change. In Austria's Justizzentrum Leoben minimum security prison, convicts live in one-bed cells which each come with a television set and en suite. Halden prison in Norway has a two-bedroom house where inmates can enjoy overnight visits from family members. Critics argue such systems can only lead to unruly
30   and dangerous behaviour, but surprisingly one of them boasts the lowest reoffending rate in Europe.

Bastøy Prison, situated on an island off the coast of Norway, is a minimum-security prison home to over 110 inmates, but only 69 staff members. Every type of offender may be accepted, and those who are [are] free to cycle the island's
35   tracks and fish in the surrounding waters. When interviewed, many of its prisoners expressed eagerness to start families and enter employment upon release.

40 Greater freedom for inmates is slowly becoming more accepted in the UK. The radio service Alan Weston wanted to listen to is part of a scheme by the Prison Radio Association, a charity established in 2006 following inmate appeals for prison radio. One of several prison programmes aimed at lowering reoffending rates, content for the Sony Award-winning NPR station is presented and produced by prisoners.

45 As the Prison Radio Association spokespeople said: 'Reducing reoffending is of benefit to everybody. Equipping prisoners with skills and confidence is crucial in bringing down reoffending rates. Prison radio offers a unique, innovative and effective way to communicate with prisoners and engage them in education, debate and community.'

50 In addition to equipping inmates for life after imprisonment, the station also gives convicts something essential to successful rehabilitation: hope. As Michael, an inmate at HMP Lindholme said: 'I've just been introduced to NPR and the inspiration your radio station gives has been a very welcome breath of fresh air. I have now found a new lease of life and I'm now going after a dream I once had as a student at college.'

55 With fewer than 15 open prisons in the UK, our system is focused on punishment rather than rehabilitation. However, the results of loosening our hold on prisoners and granting them more responsibility are clear.

SOURCE B

Corporal[1] punishment

– from a letter from Howard Livesey to *The Times*, 18 October 1888

A Crime Cure

It has been proved that imprisonment is no remedy – no adequate remedy or cure for crime. Administrators of the law have publicly given examples of criminals being sent to prison 20, 30, and even 60 times, showing the futility of confinement and the urgent need of a change of treatment. If a mode of
5 treatment was pursued in a hospital which rarely or never effected a cure, perfect or partial, the governors and subscribers would insist upon a change. As it is admitted that confinement does not cure criminals, we are cruel and culpable[2] in continuing a questionable, if not a useless formula, and withholding a remedy which might, if applied in the incipient or intermediary[3] stages of
10 criminal infection, arrest its further development. [...]

'To be kind it is sometimes needful to be cruel.' A patient is brought to a hospital, whose only chance of cure involves a terrible excision or mutilation. One of the medical staff insists upon the use of the knife, because he believes that only by it can a cure be effected, but the other members object, and so a
15 mild, painless treatment is pursued, and the man goes from bad to worse until death overtakes him. A boy is arrested for a small theft. One magistrate suggests the rod, but the others say, 'No; it will degrade him; we must not touch his body, but keep him locked up for a time,' which is done. Again this boy, now rather larger in size and in vice, comes up for sentence, say for burglary. Still his body
20 must not be touched, so he is kept a year in gaol. In a few years he is up for

highway robbery, but the Judge cannot or will not punish him bodily, but sends him abroad for a term of years. Eventually this criminal, fully developed, commits a murder; then the Judge, supported by popular consent, no longer doubtful of the propriety of paining the body – putting aside all scruples as to the justice or
25 the value of corporal punishment – sentences the prisoner to be killed!

     Thus, in the initial or premonitory symptoms of criminality – indeed, in every stage but the last – no bodily pain must be inflicted, but – when the maturity of crime is attained, the ultimatum of corporal punishment – death – is unhesitatingly enforced. Would it not be wiser and better to apply this crime
30 cure – bodily chastisement – in the first and early stages of the malady? In many cases it would probably effect a cure on the first application, and in most, if not in all, cases, it would prove effectual before the disease reached a point – the climax, at which annihilation was considered the only alternative.

     Anticipating the old, untenable objection to corporal punishment, that it
35 degrades, I observe that it is the crime and not the nature of the retribution[4] for the crime which degrades. No one would be chastised who had not degraded himself by crime. Such a sentimental and fallacious objection should not be allowed to prevent an appropriate and effective mode of punishment being applied as a crime cure to criminals, especially the young.

40 To summarise, corporal punishment is the most natural, Scriptural, and effective. The offender alone suffers for his sin. At present, wife and children often suffer more than the criminal husband or father by his incarceration. Men would not be kept from their work as breadwinners. Crime would decrease immensely, and our gaols become sparsely occupied. A vast amount of money
45 would be saved to the State, and a vast number of men restored and made good citizens.

[1]*corporal* – physical
[2]*culpable* – guilty
[3]*incipient or intermediary* – early or middle
[4]*retribution* – punishment

Section A: Reading

Answer **all** questions in this section.

You are advised to spend about 45 minutes on this section.

❶ Read again the first part of **Source A, paragraphs 1 and 2**.
Choose **four** statements on the following page which are TRUE.

  • Tick the boxes of the ones that you think are true.

  • Choose a maximum of four statements.

                                                              [4 marks]

A Eleanor Muffitt thinks the number of prisoners England and Wales is very high. ☐

B Some prisoners wander around preaching rehabilitation. ☐

C Other EU countries spend a smaller amount of their GDP on public order than the UK. ☐

D UK prison cells are cold. ☐

E UK prisons have been overcrowded for years. ☐

F Alan Weston complained that he could not access prison radio. ☐

G It is Alan Weston's first time in prison. ☐

H Experts agree that the main aim of prison should be deterrence. ☐

❷ You need to refer to **Source A** and **Source B** for this question.

Use details from **both** sources. Write a summary of their differences in attitude to dealing with crime.

[8 marks]

❸ You now need to refer **only** to **Source B**, the letter to *The Times* about corporal punishment.

How does the author, Howard Livesey, use language to argue his case?

[12 marks]

❹ For this question, you need to refer to the **whole of Source A** together with **Source B**, the letter about corporal punishment.

Compare how the two writers convey their different attitudes to dealing with crime.

In your answer, you could:

- compare their different attitudes
- compare the methods they use to convey their attitudes
- support your ideas with references to both texts.

[16 marks]

Section B: Writing

❺ You are advised to spend about 45 minutes on this section.

Write in full sentences.

You are reminded of the need to plan your answer.

You should leave enough time to check your work at the end.

'Society has a duty to help criminals to be better people, not just to punish them.'

Write an article for a broadsheet newspaper in which you explain your point of view on this statement.

(24 marks for content and organisation

16 marks for technical accuracy)

[40 marks]

PROGRESS LOG [tick the correct box]   Needs more work ☐   Getting there ☐   Under control ☐

CHAPTER 7: English Literature basics

How to use quotations

EXAM BASICS

When responding to your Literature exam questions it is important that you select appropriate quotations to support your points, and that you present the quotations effectively.

Remember:

- Keep quotations short – a few words.
- Wherever possible 'embed' your quotations.
- Use quotation marks for exact words quoted.

PRACTISE YOUR SKILLS

SELECTING QUOTATIONS

❶ Read the passage below, from *Great Expectations*, by Charles Dickens

> *I crossed the staircase landing, and entered the room she indicated. From that room, too, the daylight was completely excluded, and it had an airless smell that was oppressive. A fire had been lately kindled in the damp old-fashioned grate, and it was more disposed to go out than to burn up, and the reluctant smoke which hung in the room seemed colder than the clearer air – like our own marsh mist. Certain wintry branches of candles on the high chimney-piece faintly lighted the chamber; or it would be more expressive to say, faintly troubled its darkness. It was spacious, and I dare say had once been handsome, but every discernible thing in it was covered with dust and mould, and dropping to pieces. The most prominent object was a long table with a tablecloth spread on it, as if a feast had been in preparation when the house and the clocks all stopped together. An epergne[1] or centre-piece of some kind was in the middle of this cloth; it was so heavily overhung with cobwebs that its form was quite undistinguishable; and, as I looked along the yellow expanse out of which I remember its seeming to grow, like a black fungus, I saw speckle-legged spiders with blotchy bodies running home to it, and running out from it, as if some circumstances of the greatest public importance had just transpired in the spider community.*
>
> [1] *epergne – central table decoration*

Now, **underline words and phrases** that support the points listed below. Find at least one word or phrase for each point. Label them a–e in the extract.

a) The room is cold and comfortless.

b) The room is gloomy.

c) The narrator did not enjoy being in the room.

d) The room looks as if it was abandoned suddenly.

e) The room has long been neglected.

❷ Match each of the following **quotations** with one of the **techniques** that they could be used to illustrate. (The quotations need to be read within the context of the extract.) The first one has been done for you.

Quotation   **Technique**

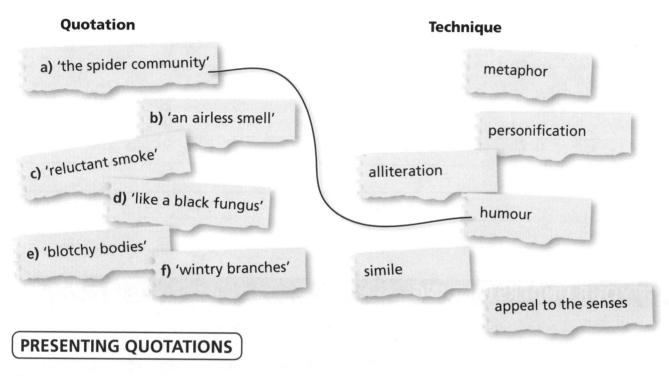

a) 'the spider community'

b) 'an airless smell'

c) 'reluctant smoke'

d) 'like a black fungus'

e) 'blotchy bodies'

f) 'wintry branches'

metaphor

personification

alliteration

humour

simile

appeal to the senses

PRESENTING QUOTATIONS

❸ Read this comment on the passage:

Dickens describes the room as large: 'spacious'. This shows the owner's wealth.

A more sophisticated approach would be to embed the quotation:

The 'spacious' room shows the owner's wealth.

Rewrite the following sentences using **embedded quotations**. Split the quotations if you wish.

a) *There is no natural light: 'daylight was completely excluded'.*

....

....

b) *The room is not up-to-date: 'old-fashioned grate'.*

....

....

c) *The narrator, Pip, may wish he was in his marshland home: 'our own marsh mist'.*

....

....

d) *Dickens hints at why the room was abandoned: 'as if a feast had been in preparation'.*

....

....

e) *The candlelight seems to make the place more gloomy: 'faintly troubled'.*

....

....

❹ You can vary the **position of quotations** in a paragraph for effect. Rearrange this statement to vary the order of **Point, Evidence and Evaluation.**

> Austen indicates that the main themes of 'Pride and Prejudice' are money and marriage by saying it is 'universally acknowledged' that a wealthy single man 'must be in want of a wife'. Her phrasing is amusingly ironic, as if she believed entirely in this so-called fact herself.

....

....

....

....

....

TEST YOUR UNDERSTANDING

❺ You might be asked a question about one of the key characters in the text you are studying. For each main point you make, you will need to provide **evidence** and **analysis/evaluation**. Use the following Point, Evidence and Evaluation about Victor Frankenstein to write an **interesting statement**. Do not use the whole quotation: select **one or two phrases.**

- Frankenstein is proud and ambitious.
- 'I will pioneer a new way, explore unknown powers, and unfold to the world the deepest mysteries of creation.' (Frankenstein)
- I think this grand language shows that he believes himself capable of godlike knowledge, and that he seeks it for the benefit of mankind.

....

....

....

....

....

....

....

....

....

....

....

PROGRESS LOG [tick the correct box]   Needs more work ▮   Getting there ▮   Under control ▮

Key themes, contexts and settings

EXAM BASICS

When writing about literature texts you should be able to show how themes are revealed and to be able to comment on the significance of context and setting.

Remember:

- Themes are major ideas explored – such as love, and money.
- Context refers to when and where a text was written, and its literary genre.
- Setting refers to when and where a text takes place (e.g. sixteenth-century Venice) or to key locations (e.g. 'a dark and dreary shop').

PRACTISE YOUR SKILLS

THEMES

❶ Which of these could be a **theme** in a text? Tick one or more boxes.

a) Liverpool ☐

b) loyalty ☐

c) a pig's head ☐

d) bullying ☐

e) appearance and reality ☐

❷ **Tick one or more** boxes to show **where** you would be more likely to find each of these themes.

Theme	Shakespeare play	Nineteenth-century novel
Kingship		
Science and technology		
Love and marriage		
The supernatural		
Education		
Revenge		
Loyalty		
Family dishonour		
Poverty and working conditions		
Class inequality		

❸ **Fill in the blanks** in the student commentary below with words from the list beneath it. You can use a word more than once.

In 'Macbeth', Shakespeare .... the theme of the .... through the Witches' predictions and the appearance of Banquo's ghost to Macbeth. In the Witches, the .... is seen as .... , because they trick Macbeth with half-truths – for example, that he cannot be killed by 'man of woman born'. In Banquo's ghost, the .... is .... to Macbeth's sense of .... , because only he can see the ghost. Yet even he cannot be sure of its reality, calling it an 'Unreal mockery'. A modern .... might be even more .... to see it in .... terms.

inclined	supernatural	linked	psychological	audience
	unreliable	explores	guilt	theme

CONTEXTS

❹ For each of the following contexts, indicate whether it is particularly relevant to **Shakespeare plays (S)** or **nineteenth-century novels (N)** by writing the appropriate letter in the box.

a) Divine Right of Kings ☐

b) decline in religious belief ☐

c) women expected to be obedient to fathers, then husbands ☐

d) belief in witchcraft ☐

e) Industrial Revolution ☐

f) Black Death (plague) ☐

g) growth of science ☐

h) interest in causes of crime ☐

i) society divided into nobility and commoners ☐

j) nature as a source of inspiration ☐

k) imperialism ☐

l) hostility towards non-Christian religions ☐

❺ Organise these sentences and part-sentences, from a student commentary on the influence of context in *Lord of the Flies*, into a **logical order** by writing the numbers 1 to 8 in the boxes.

a) and the conflict in politics between democracy and dictatorship. ☐

b) Golding was writing in the 1950s, ☐

c) In 'Lord of the Flies', Ralph represents a democratic leader, but one who lacks the charismatic appeal of Jack, whose hunting appeals more to many of the boys. ☐

d) It is an imagined nuclear war that leads to the boys being marooned without adults on the island. ☐

e) not long after the Second World War, in which he had served in the Navy. ☐

f) nuclear war because of the very different ideologies of the Communist USSR and the West. ☐

g) The novel also reflects the Cold War, when it was feared that there could be a ☐

h) The rise of Hitler, the war and concentration camps had shown the human capacity for savagery, persecution of minorities, ☐

SETTINGS

❻ Which of these is **not a setting**, or an aspect of setting? Tick one or more boxes.

- **a)** Venice ☐
- **b)** Scotland ☐
- **c)** rainy weather ☐
- **d)** the Alps ☐
- **e)** youth ☐
- **f)** the London Underground ☐
- **g)** nighttime ☐
- **h)** dishonesty ☐
- **i)** imagination ☐
- **j)** a heath ☐

TEST YOUR UNDERSTANDING

❼ Fill in this table for **three drama and prose texts** you are studying.

	Shakespeare play	Nineteenth-century novel	Modern novel/play
Title			
Main themes			
Key contexts			
Setting(s)			

PROGRESS LOG [tick the correct box] Needs more work ☐ Getting there ☐ Under control ☐

Writing about characters

EXAM BASICS

When you comment on characters you should always provide evidence for what you say.

Remember:

- Character may be implied by appearance, actions or dialogue.
- Character may be linked to themes.
- Character may be revealed by author comment, or the comments of other characters.

PRACTISE YOUR SKILLS

CHARACTERS IN SHAKESPEARE

❶ Identify the **themes** connected to the characters in these quotations. Choose from those listed below. More than one theme may apply.

a) *'A sealed bag, two sealed bags of ducats,/ Of double ducats, stolen from me by my daughter!'*
(Salanio quoting Shylock in *The Merchant of Venice*)

Theme(s) ....

b) *'… look like the innocent flower,/ But be the serpent under't'*
(Lady Macbeth advising her husband in *Macbeth*)

Theme(s) ....

c) *'Give not this rotten orange to your friend;/ She's but the sign and semblance of her honour'*
(Claudio commenting on Hero in *Much Ado About Nothing*)

Theme(s) ....

d) *'Some consequence yet hanging in the stars/ Shall bitterly begin his fearful date/ With this night's revels'*
(Romeo in *Romeo and Juliet*)

Theme(s) ....

e) *'There stand,/ For you are spell-stopp'd'*
(Prospero in *The Tempest*)

Theme(s) ....

destiny/fate	*magic*	*money*	*parenthood*
appearance and reality		*dishonour*	*marriage*

❷ How does a Shakespeare **soliloquy** give a special **insight into character**?

....

....

❸ Fill in this table for a **major character** in the **Shakespeare play** you are studying.

Character	
What do they particularly want?	
Who are their friends?	
Who are their enemies?	
Write a line that expresses their character.	
How do they change over the course of the play?	
What happens to them at the end of the play?	

SHAKESPEARE AND MODERN DRAMA

❹ Choose the **correct words** in this passage about drama.

Modern plays often give [fewer / more] character-revealing stage directions than Shakespeare. However, both follow a pattern in which characters face [facts / challenges] which eventually lead to a [disaster / dead-end / resolution]. One important thing to establish in both a Shakespeare play and a modern play is each character's [moderation / motivation / generation].

NARRATIVE VIEWPOINT IN A NOVEL

❺ On a separate sheet of paper, explain what is meant by the following:

a) first-person narrative

b) third-person narrative

c) third person but foregrounding one character

d) an unreliable narrator

e) an omniscient narrator

6 Read this student comment on Charles Dickens's *A Christmas Carol*.

> At first, Scrooge is mean and self-centred. Even in mid-winter he only has 'a very small fire', but he makes his clerk, Bob Cratchit, work with one so small 'that it looked like one coal'. He also threatens Cratchit with dismissal if he goes to put more coal on his fire. He is too mean to spend more money on coal, even to warm himself. This meanness over the fire symbolises Scrooge's lack of emotional warmth. I feel that this symbol works well because it appeals to the senses and readers can relate to it.

Use colour coding to identify the **Point, Evidence, Analysis and Evaluation** in this paragraph.

TEST YOUR UNDERSTANDING

7 Choose **three characters** from the texts you are studying. In the table below, write the name of the text and the character in the first column. For each character, write a **series of questions** that you might ask them in order to find out more about their **feelings, thoughts and motivation** – if you were able to meet them. Then write **possible answers** of one or two lines each.

Text and character	Question	Response
Shakespeare play .... Character		
Nineteenth-century novel .... Character		
Modern novel/play .... Character		

PROGRESS LOG [tick the correct box]   Needs more work ▢   Getting there ▢   Under control ▢

Key literary techniques

EXAM BASICS

When writing your response it is vital that you can identify literary techniques and analyse and evaluate the effects they create.

Remember:

- Imagery is a literary technique in which a word picture is used to make a comparison.
- A character or an object can be a symbol.
- Dramatic irony is when the audience or reader knows something that at least one character in the text does not.

PRACTISE YOUR SKILLS

IMAGERY

❶ What kind of **image** is used in each of these lines, and what is the **effect**?

a) *'like a bright squirrel'* (William Golding describing a forest fire in *Lord of the Flies*)

....

....

....

b) *'her lacquered helmet of hair'* (Meera Syal describing a woman with a beehive hairdo in *Anita and Me*)

....

....

....

c) *'that human Juggernaut trod the child down and passed on regardless of her screams'* (R. L. Stevenson describing the evil Mr Hyde in *Dr Jekyll and Mr Hyde*)

....

....

....

d) *'She [...] gave me the bread and meat without looking at me, as insolently as if I were a dog in disgrace'* (Dickens's narrator, Pip, in *Great Expectations*, describing Estella)

....

....

....

❷   What is the **effect** of **personification** in these examples?

a) *'How sweet the moonlight sleeps upon this bank!'* (Lorenzo, *The Merchant of Venice*)

....

....

b) *'Boldly they rode and well,/ Into the jaws of Death,/ Into the mouth of hell'* (Tennyson, 'The Charge of the Light Brigade')

....

....

c) *'merciless iced east winds that knive us'* (Wilfred Owen, 'Exposure')

....

....

d) *'Nor heaven peep through the blanket of the dark,/ To cry, "Hold, hold!"'* (Lady Macbeth, in *Macbeth*)

....

....

SYMBOLISM

❸   Organise the following lines into a logical **order** to make a comment on **symbolism** by writing the numbers 1 to 6 in the boxes.

a) becomes very attached to a pigeon,   ☐

b) hope, freedom, peace,   ☐

c) In *Pigeon English* the narrator, Harrison,   ☐

d) or escape from the threat of gang violence.   ☐

e) The pigeon could be seen as symbolising   ☐

f) which he tries to feed on his balcony.   ☐

❹   **Fill in the blanks** in this student commentary on Shakespeare's *Macbeth*, using words from the list below.

When .... speaks the line 'Is this a .... which I see before me', he is .... whether it is real or just 'A dagger of the mind'. For the .... , however, it is a .... of the .... Macbeth feels to carry out what he has planned with his wife: the .... of his king, Duncan. The imagined dagger could .... his desire to feel that he is being led, as if by fate, towards the murder, because he cannot at this point take .... for it.

symbol	dagger	unsure	Macbeth	audience	responsibility
	murder		temptation	represent	

DRAMATIC IRONY

❺ Which of these is an example of **dramatic irony**?

   a) In *Great Expectations*, Pip tries to put Magwitch on board a steamer on the Thames to take him out of the country, where he will be safe from the police, but he is arrested.

   b) In *Romeo and Juliet*, Romeo thinks Juliet is dead, when in fact the audience knows she has taken a sleeping potion, so he kills himself. She wakes up and finds his body beside her.

   c) In *Never Let Me Go*, the narrator becomes a carer for a terminally ill girl who once lied to her and tried to exclude her from her social friendship group.

TEST YOUR UNDERSTANDING

❻ Read this passage from *Jane Eyre*.

<u>Not a moment could be lost</u>: the very sheets were kindling. I rushed to his basin and ewer; fortunately, one was wide and the other deep, and both were filled with water. I <u>heaved</u> them up, <u>deluged</u> the bed and its occupant, <u>flew</u> back to my own room, brought my own water-jug, <u>baptised</u> the couch afresh, and, by God's aid, succeeded in extinguishing the flames which were <u>devouring</u> it.

Now complete the following task:

   a) Make **notes** commenting on the **effects** of the underlined words.

   b) Write **one or two sentences** commenting on the **effect** of the whole of the **third sentence**, from 'I heaved them up' to 'which were devouring it'.

CHAPTER 8: Paper 1: Shakespeare and the nineteenth-century novel

Section A: Shakespeare

A02

EXAM BASICS

In the exam you will be asked about an aspect of a Shakespeare play, starting with an extract. No matter what the focus of the question is, you will need to be able to show that you can analyse and evaluate Shakespeare's use of language.*

Remember:

- Stick to the question.
- Write about the extract *and* the whole play.
- Make sure that you analyse the effects of Shakespeare's language and style.

* AO2 is also assessed in other parts of the exam.

PRACTISE YOUR SKILLS

VERSE AND PROSE

❶ Underline the **correct option** in each sentence.

   a) Shakespeare's plays are [entirely / mostly / rarely] in blank verse.

   b) Commoners in Shakespeare generally speak in [verse / prose / rhyme].

   c) Blank verse means verse with no [imagery / rhythm / rhyme].

   d) A line of blank verse normally has [three / four / five] pairs of syllables.

   e) A scene often ends with a rhyming [couplet / triplet / octet].

   f) Blank verse is written in [ionic / iambic / ironic] pentameter.

❷ Which statements are **true**? Tick one or more boxes.

   a) Shakespeare's noble characters sometimes speak in prose. ☐

   b) Shakespeare's wicked characters always speak in prose. ☐

   c) Every line of Shakespeare's verse contains five syllables. ☐

   d) Occasionally Shakespeare writes in rhyming verse. ☐

   e) In blank verse, a sentence always ends at the end of a line. ☐

   f) Characters sometimes share a line of blank verse. ☐

SHAKESPEARE'S IMAGERY

❸ In this speech from *Macbeth*, the speaker, Macbeth himself, has just heard that his wife has committed suicide.

Read it, then answer the questions on a separate sheet of paper.

> *Tomorrow, and tomorrow, and tomorrow,*
> *Creeps in this petty pace from day to day*
> *To the last syllable of recorded time,*
> *And all our yesterdays have lighted fools*
> *The way to dusty death. Out, out, brief candle!*
> *Life's but a walking shadow, a poor player*
> *That struts and frets his hour upon the stage*
> *And then is heard no more: it is a tale*
> *Told by an idiot, full of sound and fury,*
> *Signifying nothing.*

a) What types of imagery does this speech use?

b) Explain what it is that 'creeps' in a 'petty pace' (slowly).

c) What is Macbeth referring to in the phase 'brief candle'?

d) What is compared with a bad actor and a stupid story, and with what effect?

❹ In this speech from *Romeo and Juliet*, Juliet's father, Capulet, tries to comfort her. He thinks she is crying over the death of her cousin Tybalt. In fact she is crying because her lover Romeo has been banished.

Read the speech, then answer the questions on a separate sheet of paper.

> *When the sun sets, the air doth drizzle dew;*
> *But for the sunset of my brother's son*
> *It rains downright.*
> *How now! A conduit,¹ girl? What, still in tears?*
> *Evermore showering? In one little body*
> *Thou counterfeit'st a bark,² a sea, a wind;*
> *For still thy eyes, which I may call the sea,*
> *Do ebb and flow with tears; the bark thy body is,*
> *Sailing in this salt flood; the winds, thy sighs;*
> *Who, raging with thy tears, and they with them,*
> *Without a sudden calm, will overset*
> *Thy tempest-tossed body.*
>
> ¹conduit – water pipe
> ²*Thou counterfeit'st a bark* – You take on the form of a ship

a) What type of image is used in 'sunset', and what does it mean?

b) With what does Capulet compare Juliet's eyes, body and sighs?

c) What type of image does Capulet use in this comparison?

d) What is Capulet's overall message to Juliet?

e) How does context influence Shakespeare's choice of imagery?

f) Explain how effective you find Capulet's attempt to comfort Juliet.

TEST YOUR UNDERSTANDING

❺ In the play you are studying, find a **blank verse speech** of at least five lines, and with at least one **image**.

  a) **Read the speech aloud** to see if each line is perfect blank verse.
     Look out for any **alterations** in rhythm or number of syllables.
     Make notes on how the verse **affects the meaning**.

  b) **Identify** the type of **imagery** used, and **analyse** how it creates **meaning**.

  c) How does the speech relate to the **rest of the play**? For example, does an **image** reflect a **theme** of the play?

Use the space below to write your notes, and then keep these notes for your revision.

Name of play: ....

Extract: Act .... Scene .... lines ....

Notes on the style of verse: ....

....

....

....

....

....

....

Notes on the imagery: ....

....

....

....

....

....

....

....

How the speech relates to the rest of the play: ....

....

....

....

....

....

....

PROGRESS LOG [tick the correct box]   Needs more work ■   Getting there ■   Under control ■

Section B: Nineteenth-century novels

A03

EXAM BASICS

In the exam you will be asked to write about an aspect of the nineteenth-century novel you have been studying, starting with an extract. A key skill in Paper 1 is to be able to comment on the significance of context and setting.*

Remember:

- Context includes the values at the time of writing, e.g. political and social concerns, and genre.
- Setting refers to when and where a text takes place (e.g. nineteenth-century London) or to key locations (e.g. an old shop).

* AO3 is also assessed in other parts of the exam.

PRACTISE YOUR SKILLS

NINETEENTH-CENTURY CONCERNS

❶   Which of these might a nineteenth-century novelist write about? Tick one or more boxes.

a) marriage and money ☐

b) science ☐

c) psychology ☐

d) social reform ☐

e) terrorism ☐

f) the role of women ☐

g) morality ☐

h) class ☐

i) genetic engineering ☐

❷   Read these two passages from nineteenth-century novels, then complete the task that follows.

> **a)** *I had saved a human being from destruction, and, as a recompense, I now writhed under the miserable pain of a wound, which shattered the flesh and bone. The feelings of kindness and gentleness which I had entertained but a few moments before gave place to hellish rage and gnashing of teeth. Inflamed by pain, I vowed eternal hatred and vengeance to all mankind.*
>
> (The Monster in Mary Shelley's *Frankenstein*)

> **b)** *Evil besides (which I must still believe to be the lethal side of man) had left on that body an imprint of deformity and decay. And yet when I looked upon that ugly idol in the glass, I was conscious of no repugnance, rather of a leap of welcome. This, too, was myself. It seemed natural and human. [...] I have observed that when I wore the semblance of Edward Hyde, none could come near to me at first without a visible misgiving of the flesh. This, as I take it, was because all human beings, as we meet them, are commingled out of good and evil: and Edward Hyde, alone in the ranks of mankind, was pure evil.*
>
> (R. L. Stevenson, *The Strange Case of Dr Jekyll and Mr Hyde*)

Both of these texts are concerned with the idea of **goodness and compassion** versus **self-centredness and evil** – and the **balance** of the two in mankind.

Summarise what each of these paragraphs seems to say about this theme.

a) ....

....

b) ....

....

SOCIAL CONDITIONS

❸   What **social conditions** are reflected in each of these passages?
(Passage **c)** is on page 85.)

> **a)** *'Younger sons cannot marry where they like.'*
> *'Unless where they like women of fortune, which I think they very often do.'*
> *'Our habits of expense make us too dependent, and there are not many in my rank of life who can afford to marry without some attention to money.'*
>
> (Colonel Fitzwilliam and Elizabeth discuss marriage in *Pride and Prejudice*)

....

....

....

....

> **b)** *I've been done everything to, pretty well – except hanged. I've been locked up, as much as a silver tea-kittle.[1] I've been carted here and carted there, and put out of this town, and put out of that town, and stuck in the stocks, and whipped and worried and drove. [...] I got the name of being hardened. 'This is a terrible hardened one,' they says to prison wisitors, picking out me. 'May be said to live in jails, this boy.'*
>
> [1] *kittle* – how Magwitch pronounces 'kettle'; see also 'wisitors' for 'visitors'
>
> (Magwitch describes his early years in *Great Expectations*)

....

....

....

....

c) 'You shall go to a place I have in the south of France: a whitewashed villa on the shores of the Mediterranean. There you shall live a happy, and guarded, and most innocent life.' [...]

'Sir, your wife is living: that is a fact acknowledged this morning by yourself. If I lived with you as you desire, I should then be your mistress: to say otherwise is sophistical – is false.'

(Jane refuses to live with Rochester, because he is already married, in *Jane Eyre*)

....

....

....

....

TEST YOUR UNDERSTANDING

4 In the table below, make notes on **three important characters** in the novel you are studying. Consider:

    a) How he/she **reflects nineteenth-century concerns**

    b) How he/she is **affected by nineteenth-century social conditions**

Character	Reflects concerns	Affected by conditions

CHAPTER 9: Paper 2, Section A: Modern prose and drama

Modern prose

EXAM BASICS

In Paper 2, you will be given a choice of two questions on your modern set text. If you are studying a modern prose text the questions might focus on a character or be theme-based. Whatever type of question you answer, you will need to analyse and evaluate the author's use of language and context.

Remember:

- Answer the exact question that is asked.
- Analyse and evaluate the writer's techniques.
- Show that you understand the role of the character or theme.

PRACTISE YOUR SKILLS

CHARACTERISATION

❶ Read this extract from a piece of modern fiction.

> *She glimpsed Dan's face, scowling as usual, through the window. In a moment he burst through the door and slammed it behind him. Such selfish indifference: surely he knew that their mother was trying to sleep upstairs.*
>
> *'Get out of it!' he growled at the family labrador, aiming a kick that barely missed the cowering animal. 'And what are you staring at, woman?'*

a) What key elements of **characterisation** are used here?

....

....

....

b) What **narrative viewpoint** is used by the writer?

....

....

....

❷ Which of these is a difficulty that an author must overcome if using a **first-person narrator**? Tick one or more boxes.

a) It is only possible to write about one character in depth. ☐

b) The narrator can only describe what they actually witness or hear about. ☐

c) First-person narrators are always unreliable. ☐

d) A narrator cannot describe themselves as easily as an author can in the third person. ☐

e) The narrator cannot take part in dialogue. ☐

❸ How is **narrative viewpoint** used in the passage below?

> *He walked down the narrow path to the river, cautiously ducking the long tendrils of bramble that dangled in the way. He must remember to bring shears next time he came. He was lost in thoughts of Jenny when he heard the gate creak open and shut.*

....

....

....

❹ How do the author's **word choices** imply **character** in this passage?

> *He stared at her unblinking through steel-rimmed spectacles.*
> *'I –' she began, but he raised a bony hand like a police road block to silence her.*
> *He spoke precisely, dividing his words into neat, impersonal parcels. 'I'm afraid we shan't been requiring your services anymore.' His voice was like dead grass in a cold wind. 'You are no longer necessary.'*
> *He brushed a speck of dust from his papers and began to study them, and, after a few moments, she realised that the interview was over.*

....

....

....

....

....

MODERN THEMES

❺ These are some of the **themes** in the modern prose texts on the AQA specification. On a separate piece of paper, explain which ones relate to the text you are studying, and how.

a) social duty

b) friendship

c) creativity

d) prejudice

e) peer pressure

f) human capacity for evil

g) power and leadership

h) deception

i) abuse of science

j) the individual's role in society

k) family

l) cultural identity

m) love

n) being an outsider

o) bereavement

p) war

❻ **Themes** in modern prose texts often **connect or overlap**. For example, in *Lord of the Flies* there is peer pressure to give in to evil.

On a separate piece of paper, list or make a **spidergram or mind map** of the **themes** in the novel/short story anthology you are studying. Then draw lines between those that you think are **connected**. Make **notes** on whichever you think is the most important **theme connection** in your novel/anthology.

TEST YOUR UNDERSTANDING

❼ Find a passage of about twenty lines in your novel (or short story from the Anthology) that you like, or choose it randomly.

For this passage, make notes on the following:

a) How one or more **characters** are presented (think of **description, action and dialogue**)

b) What **themes** are suggested

c) **How this passage fits** into the whole novel or short story – for example, do the characters go on to change dramatically, or are the themes developed?

Use the space below to write your notes.

....

....

....

....

....

....

....

....

....

....

....

....

....

....

....

....

....

....

....

....

....

....

....

....

....

....

PROGRESS LOG [tick the correct box]   Needs more work ▢   Getting there ▢   Under control ▢

Modern drama

A01 **A02** **A03**

PAPER 2,
SECTION A

EXAM BASICS

If you are studying a modern drama text, it is likely you will be asked a question on a character or a theme. Whichever type of question you answer, you will need to show the examiner that you can analyse and evaluate the author's use of language and context.

Remember:

- Answer the exact question that is asked.
- Analyse and evaluate the dramatist's techniques.
- Show that you understand the role of the character or theme.

PRACTISE YOUR SKILLS

DRAMATIC FORM

❶ Which of the following feature in the modern play you are studying? Tick one or more boxes.

   a) detailed, precise stage directions   ☐

   b) a narrator   ☐

   c) more than one setting   ☐

   d) an important character who never appears on stage   ☐

   e) takes place over a long period of time   ☐

   f) a flashback in time   ☐

   g) a 'play within a play'   ☐

   h) prologue or epilogue   ☐

❷ **Five-point story design** is one way to understand the structure of a play. Put its elements in the correct order by writing the numbers 1 to 5 in the boxes.

   a) successes and reverses   ☐

   b) the inciting incident or trigger   ☐

   c) resolution   ☐

   d) climax   ☐

   e) crisis   ☐

❸ Using the table below and on page 90, explain how each of these **stages** in **five-point story design** relates to the play you are studying.

Stage	How it relates to your play

❹ In *Blood Brothers* there is a scene in which twin boys, separated at birth, meet by accident, become friends and decide to become 'blood brothers'. The audience knows that they already are 'blood brothers', but *they* do not.

   a) What name is given to this **dramatic technique**?

   b) Can you find an **example of this technique** in the play you are studying (or another example if your play is *Blood Brothers*)?

   c) How do you think an **audience** might be **affected** by the use of this technique?

❺ Which of the following can be achieved using **stage directions**? Tick one or more boxes.

   a) setting the scene   ☐

   b) describing how characters look or speak   ☐

   c) explaining dialogue   ☐

   d) hinting at characterisation   ☐

   e) giving the author's political views   ☐

❻ A play may **create mood** by using just one **setting** (as in *An Inspector Calls*), or by contrasting two or more settings. Write a sentence about the importance of setting in the play you are studying.

....

....

....

7 Read this example of **dramatic sub-text** and answer the questions on a separate piece of paper.

> (Inspector Goole has just entered to interview the Birling family in *An Inspector Calls*.)
>
> *Birling*: You're new aren't you?
>
> *Inspector*: Yes, sir. Only recently transferred.
>
> *Birling*: I thought you must be. I was an alderman for years – and Lord Mayor two years ago – and I'm still on the Bench[1] – so I know the Brumley police officers pretty well – and I thought I'd never seen you before.
>
> [1]*Bench* – magistrate's court   = a judge

a) **Explain** how 'sub-text' works in this piece of dialogue.

b) Explain the probable <u>underlying meaning</u> of each line. (You could write it on the script itself.)

c) Find and make notes on a short piece of dialogue in the play you are studying in which two speakers **do not mean exactly what they are saying**. **Analyse** what you think they mean.

TEST YOUR UNDERSTANDING

8 Choose one **extract** from the play you are studying and write a **paragraph** explaining the following:

- How it fits into the **structure** of the play
- How **stage directions** (if any) are used
- The importance of its **setting**
- What it reveals about **characters** and in what ways
- What the **characters** in the extract **really want**, and how this is **hinted at** (if at all) in the extract

....
....
....
....
....
....
....
....
....
....
....
....

PROGRESS LOG [tick the correct box]   Needs more work ☐   Getting there ☐   Under control ☐

CHAPTER 10: Paper 2, Sections B and C: Poetry

Section B: Poetic techniques

PAPER 2,
SECTION B

EXAM BASICS

In Paper 2, Section B you will be asked to compare how two poems from your Anthology cluster present a subject or theme. You must ensure that you analyse and evaluate the poets' use of language.

Remember:

- Focus on the subject or theme in the question.
- Do not just point out poetic techniques – analyse and evaluate them.
- Comment on detail and overall structure.

PRACTISE YOUR SKILLS

RHYTHM, METRE AND RHYME

❶ Read each of the poem extracts below aloud in a natural way. **Tap out** the **rhythm** as you speak. Then **underline** the **stressed** (emphasised) syllables. Finally, comment on how the **rhythm matches the sense** in each extract.

> **a)** *'My name is Ozymandias, king of kings:*
> *Look on my works, ye Mighty, and despair!'*
>
> Percy Bysshe Shelley, 'Ozymandias'
>
> **b)** *Slowly our ghosts drag home: glimpsing the sunk fires, glozed[1]*
> *With crusted dark-red jewels; crickets jingle there*
>
> Wilfred Owen, 'Exposure'
>
> [1] *glozed* – glossed, shining

In 'Ozymandias', the ....

....

....

In 'Exposure', the ....

....

....

❷ The most common metre in English is **iambic pentameter**.

   a) What is iambic pentameter? ....

   ....

b) Are there any poems in the anthology you are studying that are written in iambic pentameter? If so, which? ....

....

❸ Read this part of a stanza from Lord Byron's 'When We Two Parted' and answer the questions that follow.

> *The dew of the morning*
> *Sunk chill on my brow –*
> *It felt like the warning*
> *Of what I feel now*

a) How many **stresses** are there in each line? (Read the extract aloud and mark them.)

b) What is the **rhyme scheme**? (Use letters – A, B, C, etc. – to identify it.)

c) What **mood** does the rhythm and rhyme help to reinforce?

....

....

....

❹ Read this stanza from Wilfred Owen's 'Exposure' and answer the questions that follow.

> *Watching, we hear the mad gusts tugging on the wire,*
> *Like twitching agonies of men among its brambles.*
> *Northward, incessantly, the flickering gunnery rumbles,*
> *Far off, like a dull rumour of some other war.*
> *   What are we doing here?*

a) Circle and link the **half-rhymes** at the end of the lines.

b) Tick the correct box to indicate which you think is the most likely reason for Owen using these half-rhymes.

They create a sense of uneasiness and incompletion.	☐
He does not want the rhymes to be too obvious.	☐
He could not find better rhymes for these words.	☐
They are depressing.	☐

IMAGERY

❺ What **images** are used in these extracts, and what is their **effect**? Write your answers on a separate piece of paper.

> **a)** *I think of thee! – my thoughts do twine and bud*
> *About thee, as wild vines, about a tree,*
> *Put out broad leaves*
>
> E. B. Browning, Sonnet 29 – 'I think of thee'
>
> **b)** *a huge peak, black and huge,*
> *As if with voluntary power instinct,*
> *Upreared its head*
>
> William Wordsworth, 'Extract from *The Prelude*'

ALLITERATION

6 Underline the words creating **alliteration** in these extracts, and suggest what **effect** each of the examples has.

> **a)** _her cheek once more_
> _Blushed bright beneath my burning kiss:_
> _I propped her head up as before_
>
> Robert Browning, 'Porphyria's Lover'
>
> **b)** _In every voice, in every ban,_
> _The mind-forg'd manacles I hear_
>
> William Blake, 'London'

In 'Porphyria's Lover', ...

....

....

In 'London', the ....

....

....

TEST YOUR UNDERSTANDING

7 Choose two poems in the cluster you are studying. For each poem, make notes below on the following, including their effects:

- **Rhythm** (and metre if used) and **rhyme**
- **Imagery**
- **Alliteration**

Then, on a separate piece of paper, write **one or two paragraphs comparing** these features in both poems.

....

....

....

....

....

....

....

....

....

....

PROGRESS LOG [tick the correct box] Needs more work ☐ Getting there ☐ Under control ☐

Section C: Reading an unseen poem

A01 A02

EXAM BASICS

In Paper 2, Section C you will be asked to answer a question about how the poet presents feelings or ideas in an unseen poem. You will need to analyse the poet's use of language.

Remember:

- Annotate the poem and make notes before you start writing.
- Look for the 'story' of the poem, and any elements of location.
- See how imagery and techniques express the poet's feelings about the subject.

PRACTISE YOUR SKILLS

First, read this poem, by D. H. Lawrence. Bear in mind the following question and then complete Tasks 1–10. (You may find it useful to copy the poem onto a large piece of paper.)

How does the poet present his feelings about the storm and nature as a whole?

> **Storm in the Black Forest**
>
> *Now it is almost night, from the bronzey soft sky*
> *jugfull after jugfull of pure white liquid fire, bright white*
> *tipples over and spills down,*
> *and is gone*
> *and gold-bronze flutters bent through the thick upper air*
>
> *And as the electric liquid pours out, sometimes*
> *a still brighter white snake wriggles among it, spilled*
> *and tumbling wriggling down the sky:*
> *and then the heavens cackle with unicorn sounds.*
>
> *And the rain won't come, the rain refuses to come!*
>
> *This is the electricity that man is supposed to have mastered*
> *chained, subjugated to his use!*
>
> *supposed to!*

THE TITLE AND 'STORY' OF THE POEM

❶ **Underline** the phrase in the title that tells us **where** the poem is set. You might also like to look this place up.

❷ **Underline** the phrase in the poem that tells us **when** (what time of day) the poem is set. How does this affect the **mood** of the poem?

❸ Underline key words to indicate **what Lawrence sees**. Then add numbers to indicate the stages of his description. Include the surprising **'non-event'** at the end of stanza 2, and write a note on it.

❹ Add a note next to the **final three lines** explaining in a few words what **conclusion** Lawrence seems to reach – the end of the poem's 'story'.

IMAGERY

❺ **Underline or colour-code** all the **images** you can find in the poem. Write them on a separate sheet of plain paper and use **spidergrams or mind maps** to explore your own **associations** with these things.

For example, you might begin with 'JUGFULL' in the middle and ideas branching off, such as 'MILK JUG', 'ENDLESS SUPPLY' and 'NOURISHING'.

Write down what **type of image** they are, e.g. metaphor.

VISUAL/AUDITORY APPEAL AND WORD CHOICES

❻ Underline Lawrence's **use of colour** (including white). Add a note on the **effect**.

❼ **Underline** these **verbs** in the poem:

> tipples   spills   flutters   pours
> wriggles/wriggling   tumbling

a) What do these **words suggest** to you individually? (You could write them out spread over a sheet of paper and add your associations around them.)

b) What **overall impression** do they give of the **lightning**?

❽ What **effect** is created in the final stanza by the words 'mastered / chained, subjugated'?

....

....

....

....

❾ What words does Lawrence **repeat**, and what is the **effect**?

....

....

....

....

TEST YOUR UNDERSTANDING

⑩ Use your **annotations** to help you write an **analysis and evaluation** of the poem. Include:

- The basic **'story'** – what the poem is about and how it concludes
- What **imagery** is used and its **effect**
- How the poem **appeals to the senses** – and how this expresses Lawrence's **feelings** about the **storm**, and **nature**
- How **word choices** (especially verbs) and **repetition** create **effects**, individually and overall
- Your view of the poem's overall **'message'**, and how the **language** conveys it

....

....

....

....

....

....

....

....

....

....

....

....

....

....

....

....

....

....

....

....

....

....

....

....

....

....

....

PROGRESS LOG [tick the correct box]   Needs more work ■   Getting there ■   Under control ■

Sections B and C: Comparing poems (A01) (A02) (A03)

EXAM BASICS

In both Sections B and C you will be asked to compare how two poems present attitudes or feelings about a subject or theme. The following few pages focus on Section B and the Anthology poems, but the tasks are also useful preparation for comparing two unseen poems in Section C. For example, you could complete tasks on poems from the other cluster to practise comparing unseen poems.

Remember:

● Annotate the poem(s) before you start writing.
● Look for similarities and differences in language, structure and form.
● Compare the poems' effects on the reader.

PRACTISE YOUR SKILLS

CHOOSING CLUSTER POEMS TO COMPARE

❶ **a)** If you are studying the 'Love and relationships' cluster, make a five-column table listing all the poems in the first column. Head columns 2–5 as follows:

	Romantic love	Separation, loss	Family love	Memory and time

Think carefully about the **themes** of each poem. Then tick boxes in your table to indicate them – as many as you think are relevant.

b) Or, if you are studying the 'Power and conflict' cluster, make a seven-column table listing all the poems in the left-hand column. Head columns 2–7 as follows:

	War, soldiers	Political power	Patriotism	Death, loss	Nature	Inner conflict

Think carefully about the **themes** of each poem. Then tick boxes in your table to indicate them – as many as you think are relevant.

❷ Based on your entries in the **themes** table, consider what poems you would choose to **compare** with *either*:

a) (Love and relationships) 'Porphyria's Lover' or 'Eden Rock'

or

b) (Power and conflict) 'Ozymandias' or 'Bayonet Charge'

'STORY' AND ATTITUDES

❸ Read 'Mother, Any Distance' and 'Before You Were Mine' in your Anthology. On a separate piece of paper, make notes on:

   a) How each poet seems to view their **mother**

   b) How they use **language** to convey their **feelings**

❹ Read 'Remains' and 'War Photographer' in your Anthology. Again using a separate piece of paper, make notes on:

   a) How the **'story'** is told in each case

   b) How each of them is **damaged** by their experience of **war**, and how **language** is used to convey this damage

COMPARING VERSE FORM

❺ Read 'The Charge of the Light Brigade' and 'Checking Out Me History' in your Anthology.

   a) Explain **why**, in your view, Tennyson **rhymes** several different words with 'hundred' (e.g. 'blunder'd').

....

....

....

   b) Explain **why**, in your view, Agard **rhymes** all four lines in the fifth stanza (lines 22–5).

....

....

....

❻ Read 'When We Two Parted' and 'Singh Song!' in your Anthology.

   a) What **tense** is used in each poem, and what is the **effect**?

....

....

....

   b) Compare the **effects** of **rhythm** in stanza 1 of 'When We Two Parted' and stanza 3 of 'Singh Song!'

....

....

....

   c) Compare the use of **rhyme** in 'When We Two Parted' stanza 2 and 'Singh Song!' stanza 2.

....

....

....

COMPARING IMAGERY

❼ Referring to your Anthology:

a) Compare the use of **imagery** to convey the **feelings** involved in a **relationship** in 'Neutral Tones' stanza 3 and 'Winter Swans' stanza 4.

b) Compare the use of **imagery** to describe **nature** in 'Extract from *The Prelude*' lines 25–9 and the last five lines of 'Storm on the Island'.

Use a separate piece of paper for this task.

TEST YOUR UNDERSTANDING

❽ Write **one or two paragraphs** comparing **'story'** and **attitudes, verse form** and **imagery** in two poems.

a) For 'Love and relationships', compare 'Porphyria's Lover' and another poem in the Anthology that you think has some similarities in theme.

b) For 'Power and conflict', compare 'London' and another poem in the Anthology that you think has some similarities in theme.

....
....
....
....
....
....
....
....
....
....
....
....
....
....
....
....
....
....
....
....

PROGRESS LOG [tick the correct box]   Needs more work ☐   Getting there ☐   Under control ☐

PART ONE: THE BASICS

CHAPTER 1 [pp. 6–11]

Spelling [p. 6]

1

a) beliefs cherries chiefs churches
b) cuffs dairies donkeys fairies
c) foxes glasses journeys scarves
d) knives lorries monkeys peaches
e) ruffs trays wharves wolves

2

a) unacceptable irregular unnecessary impolite
b) unintelligent uncaring inefficient ineligible
c) imprecise inappropriate inedible unequal

3

a) noticeable
b) accessible
c) manageable
d) legible
e) excitable
f) divisible

4 always beautifully almost hopeful impressive beautiful penniless until worrisome

5 When I went to see the **principal**, she said she would **write** me a letter on her own **stationery** so that I **would** be **allowed** to miss Games.

'**It's** not often I do this,' she said. '**It's** a question of **principle**. I only do it for someone **who's** got a genuine excuse – for example, **their** health is poor and **they're** in danger of it getting worse. I don't know **whether** you realise that. Anyway, **it's too** late for Games now, so this letter may have already lost **its** usefulness.'

As I walked to the changing rooms, I felt relieved. My excuse had been **accepted**. Everything was fine – **except** that I couldn't think **where** the letter had got to!

Sentences and grammar [p. 8]

1

a) Aled, who is a plumber by trade, is very practical.
b) Aberdeen, which is a long way north, gets very cold in winter.
c) I was brought up in Calcutta, which is a huge city.

2

a) She had bought a ticket. She felt she might as well go to the concert.
b) Amir preferred football to Maths. He stayed away.
c) I scored once. That is more than Wayne ever manages.

3

a) I opened the safe. Empty!
b) It was silent. Apart from the beating of my heart.
c) There was nothing but rain. All day!

4 Rushing to the river, I jumped in and swam across. The freezing water took my breath away as if it had been sucked out of me, but I made it to the other side. I just had time to look back: they were still pursuing me. There was a puff of smoke from a rifle, and a crack like a branch breaking, followed by the ricochet of a bullet off the rocks a foot away from me. I put my head down and ran.

5

a) We can have <u>whatever we want</u>.
b) Give the prize to <u>whoever arrives first</u>.
c) <u>What you see</u> is what you get.

6

a) Fatima, <u>who lives in Peckham</u>, had to take the bus.
b) We watched *Peaky Blinders*, <u>which is set in Birmingham</u>.
c) China, <u>which has a fast-growing economy</u>, objected.

7

a) You'll need a thermal jacket <u>if you're going to avoid freezing</u>.
b) <u>To stalk the seal</u>, the polar bear swims underwater.
c) I'm going to let you off this time <u>because of your previous good behaviour</u>.

8

a) The runners **were** approaching the finish.
b) A flock of sheep **has** wandered on to the road.
c) The wolf pack **is** hunting a bison.

9

a) What would you say if I <u>sang</u> out of tune?
b) If I <u>were</u> to complain, I would only annoy them.
c) If I <u>bought</u> these jeans now, would you change them if necessary?

Punctuation [p. 10]

1

a) After eating, Kevin, Ian and Ravi went to the park.
b) Malachi, who is doing Media Studies, directed the video.
c) Sue who works in Boots came to the party, but Sue who's in our class didn't.

2

a) Rain, snow and sleet, along with black ice, are some of the road hazards today.
b) The current stars of *TOWIE*, *Coronation Street* and *EastEnders*, and a few from *Emmerdale*, *Hollyoaks* and *Home and Away*, attended the event.
c) She ordered a sandwich with salmon, cream cheese and cucumber, and waited.

3 Lines b) and d) – a) and c) incorrectly use a comma splice.

4 a) and c)

5

a) There is only one reason to shop at Betterbuy: it's cheap.
b) Dogs are obedient, loving and loyal; cats will cuddle up to anyone who feeds them.
c) We took the following: ropes, flexible ladders and clips; sandwiches, drinks and snacks; and a range of maps.

6

a) Egypt – with the Nile, tombs and pyramids – is one of the most popular destinations.
b) I have one relative – a cousin, but I last saw him two years ago.
c) You – of all people – should understand.

7

a) 'Desiree', he insisted, 'is the only girl for me.'
b) 'Once upon a time,' I began, 'there was a little girl called Goldilocks.'
c) I stared hard at him. 'Who do you think you're fooling?' I said. 'Not me, for one.'

8

a) My great-grandfather drove a Centurion (a kind of tank) in the war.
b) I listed the things I needed: flour (plain), sugar (brown), butter (or margarine) and a lemon.
c) Panamanians (most of them) are Spanish-speaking.

9 It was a sunny afternoon in the park. James, Darrel and Omar were kicking a ball around; Emma and Sita were sitting on the grass texting.

Emma looked up from her phone when a buzzing noise distracted her. She thought at first it was a large bee: she hated bees, having been stung once.

Sita heard it, too. 'What's that?' she said, looking around. 'That buzzing.'

The boys had stopped their game, though it had hardly been a proper game in the first place – there were only three of them.

'Look,' said Darrel, pointing up. 'It's a tiny spaceship!'

'Don't be daft,' said Omar. 'I'll tell you what it is – a drone. They're being used to deliver parcels now.'

'Well, do you really think that one's delivering a parcel?' said Darrel. 'I think it's spying on us. Probably scouting for new talent!'

PART TWO: GCSE ENGLISH LANGUAGE [pp. 12–67]

CHAPTER 2 [pp. 12–25]

Identifying information [p. 12]

1 Answer d) is correct. Answer a) is wrong because Bellows did not actually see it. Answer b) is wrong because we do not know that he is definitely a student: he may be a teacher. Answer c) is wrong because there is no mention of a window. The sound of breaking glass probably comes from something Davidson has knocked over.

2 Possible answers (four of the following): Bellows was the first to arrive after Davidson had a seizure. The incident occurred at Harlow Technical College. Davidson was alone when he had the seizure. The balances are kept in the smaller of the two rooms. The thunderstorm had upset Bellows's work. The hail was noisy on the corrugated roof. There was a loud smash. Something had been knocked off the bench.

3 Possible answers:

a) He is puzzled by his experience (*a queer sort of laugh* […] *dazzled*).

b) He cannot see, or is unaware of, Bellows (*He did not notice me*).

c) He can see, or thinks he can see, something that Bellows cannot see (*clawing out at something invisible*).

d) He wants to discover whether he can see his own hand (*He held up his hands to his face*).

4

a) He appears to be inebriated.

b) He grabs at the air.

5

a) Davidson thinks that Bellows is hiding.

b) Davidson cannot see Bellows.

c) Davidson feels afraid and threatened.

d) Davidson decides to escape the threat he perceives.

Analysing language features [p. 15]

1

- 'beautiful […] splendid' – He appreciates their beauty and likely cost.
- 'crimson' – A colour associated with wealth and royalty: he sees the inhabitants as wealthy.
- 'pure white' – He thinks the owners can afford to keep the house clean and freshly painted; also suggests purity.

- 'gold' – he thinks the owners are wealthy.
- 'shower of glass-drops' – Metaphor implying his wonder at seeing a chandelier for the first time.
- 'shimmering with little soft tapers' – He finds it beautiful and delicate. The delicacy and softness would suggest to him the refinement and softness of a wealthy family who do not have to work.

2 The boy responds to seeing the sword as if it is something magical, and which gives out a magical 'flash of light'. He is utterly amazed ('transfixed') by its appearance, his mouth 'gaping' in disbelief. Together these descriptions suggest a world that hypnotises him.

3 They are short simple sentences, and the second is a minor sentence.

4 They create a dramatic sense of the boy being told he cannot hold the sword – as if an adult has told him abruptly, as if no further explanation is needed. The minor sentence, especially, implies that the boy disapproves of this ban.

5 Pray, don't imagine that he conceals depths [e] of benevolence and affection beneath a stern exterior [d] ! He's not a rough diamond [e] – [a] a pearl-containing oyster [e] of a rustic: he's a fierce, pitiless, wolfish [b] man! … [He'd] crush you like a sparrow's egg. [c]

6 In this passage, Heathcliff is presented as a violent character who will destroy a weaker person if it pleases him. It also suggests that Isabella mustn't be deceived into thinking he is capable of love and goodwill.

7 Heathcliff's use of the word 'unutterable' shows that he finds Catherine's death almost too terrible to speak about. His exclamations, repeating 'I *cannot* live without', show his desperation, and calling her his 'life' and 'soul' show how bound to her he feels. His violent behaviour, together with the violent verbs 'dashed' and 'thundered' show his strong feeling. To the narrator, he seems like an animal, 'howling' like a wolf or some other 'savage beast', showing that he has been reduced to a raw emotion that is deeper than anything civilised – almost beyond being human.

Understanding structures [p. 18]

1

a) addressing the reader – A
b) giving a strong sense of setting – B
c) raising questions about a character's daily life – A
d) raising questions as to why a character is where they are – B

2 Important elements of structure: a), c), d), h), i)

3

a) The passage follows the man's view, focusing in on the door.
b) It makes the reader want to know why the door will 'fly open', and who or what will emerge.
c) It uses a 'flashback', and identifies the point in time that led directly to the man's present predicament.
d) It returns to the present moment with a bang – literally.

4 The passage begins with the sense of hearing, describing sounds as the wind drops. It then shifts to the sight of the sail, from James's viewpoint, and the boat being becalmed (not moving). Everything stops, and the people in the boat become more aware of each other – all except for one, as the narrator zooms in on Mr Ramsay.

Evaluating characters, themes and settings [p. 21]

1

a) 'lips whose remarkable ruddiness showed astonishing vitality'
b) 'a strong – a very strong – aquiline'; 'the chin was broad and strong'
c) 'extraordinary pallor'
d) 'massive' eyebrows; 'cruel-looking' mouth
e) 'hairs in the centre of the palm'
f) 'peculiarly sharp white teeth; these protruded over the lips'; nails 'cut to a sharp point'

2

a) The verbs 'ripped', 'stabbed', 'squashed', 'scraping' and 'sawed' suggest anger and aggression; 'glared', 'snorted' and 'scowl' suggest a critical, disapproving character. The formal 'requested' implies a demanding, unforgiving nature. 'Sawing' also implies that he is making a show of the effort he has to make, as if he wants his wife to feel guilty.
b) His folded arms convey a refusal to accept the situation: he is not an easy-going man. His impatient gesturing confirms this. The way he rips open the butter and spreads it is violent, but also childish, as if he wants to create a drama. His pausing to 'scowl' at his wife before eating suggests that he wants to make an impact, as if punishing her for suggesting that he is making a fuss. Calling the staff 'idiots' is judgemental, and his detailed account of his order makes him sound very exacting.

3

a) listing: The list of things that other people have, 'glossy jobs in glass-fronted offices; lunch dates with eager friends in cosy bars; heated homes …', emphasises what Ellie longs to have.
b) short and incomplete sentences: 'Her? Empty pockets, boots in holes, ripped jacket. She shivered', shows the stark reality of Ellie's

situation. The minimal sentences reflect how little she has.

c) contrast: Ellie's poverty and her shivering alone in the cold as an outsider are contrasted with people having jobs, meeting friends, or living in warm, comfortable homes. Her threadbare appearance is contrasted with that of the elegant woman.

d) revealing details: Ellie's clothes and cup show her situation starkly; the luxurious details describing the woman show how fortunate she is by comparison.

e) different viewpoints: The phrase 'That was when she knew it ...' expresses Ellie's viewpoint; the final sentence shows the viewpoint of the passers-by.'

4 The details describing Ellie's 'threadbare knees', 'empty pockets, boots with holes' and 'ripped jacket' show how poor she is. Her state is effectively contrasted with that of the elegant woman in an expensive coat and jewellery. When the woman glances away, she is probably trying to ignore Ellie. The simile comparing Ellie to a ghost shows how people fail to recognise her as a fellow human being.

5 a), b), c), e), f)

6

a) Helps to create an appropriate **mood** – such as tense, relaxed, menacing.
b) Prepares the reader for a particular sort of **action**.
c) Helps the reader to **imagine** where the action takes place.
d) Can be associated with a major **character** – e.g. Dracula and his castle.
e) Can include place, time of day and **weather**.

7 The setting creates a sense of menace, particularly the 'ghastly' tombs and gloomy trees, described as 'funereal'. Even the sounds of nature and the dogs seem threatening. Both the adverb 'ominously' and the phrase 'woeful presage' (a dire warning sign) make the reader expect the worst. This prepares us for the frightening moment when the woman appears. The description of her changing from 'a dim white figure' to being suddenly shown by the moonlight in 'startling prominence' makes this dramatic.

8 c)

9 Fliss does not share Aaron's enthusiasm. [**Point**] Her 'surveying the scene with distaste', her 'folded' arms and her remaining 'on the perimeter' [**Evidence**] all indicate her refusal to get involved. [**Analysis**]

10 The way Fliss stands 'surveying the scene with distaste', 'arms folded' , 'on the perimeter ...' [**Evidence**] all indicate her refusal to get involved, [**Analysis**] revealing that she does not share Aaron's enthusiasm. [**Point**] The use of body language is an effective way to show this. [**Evaluation**]

11 The writer's language presents Aaron as someone full of energy. The verbs 'darted', 'leapt', 'peering' and 'pausing' are chosen to show how active he is, spurred on by his enthusiasm. The alliteration in 'toss [...] or tuck' emphasises this, as well as his quick decision-making.

He certainly sees the dump as an opportunity, as suggested by 'kingdom', 'perfume of possibility' and 'treasure trove'. The choice of 'perfume' in connection with a rubbish dump is particularly effective, because it is surprising. The alliteration links the two words 'perfume' and 'possibility'.

Aaron's exclamation 'Whoah!' shows his enthusiasm, as does his list of three – 'toasters, radios, the lot'. He is clearly so 'eager' about his find that he does not even mind kneeling on a 'sodden carpet' to look at it more closely.

CHAPTER 3 [pp. 26–37]

Describing setting and creating atmosphere [p. 26]

1 Suggested answers:

biting east wind [c] coconut palms [a] beach balls [b] deckchairs jammed together [b]

hypnotic sound of surf [a] shingle [c] rock pools with starfish [a] jagged rocks [c]

inflatables [b] melting ice cream [b] gentle breeze [a] tide-ribbed sand [c]

looming clouds [c] pelicans flying overhead [a] sandcastles [b]

2

a) The cold east wind <u>slices</u> right through her thin jacket.
b) Pelicans <u>flapped</u> lazily over the blue lagoon.
c) In the storm, huge waves <u>dashed</u> against the jagged rocks.
d) It was a perfect day for relaxing on the beach. A faint breeze <u>fanned</u> the coconut palms.

3

a) The dungeon was dark and felt unhealthily <u>dank</u> after the fresh summer air outside.
b) Jungle creepers coil round the trees like <u>writhing</u> snakes.
c) A fresh layer of <u>powdery</u> snow lay on the ground.
d) She needed to get above the flood, but the walls of the tower were <u>unscalable</u>.

4 Suggested answer:

The river <u>snaked</u> around the promontory, lapping like <u>a jaguar</u> at its slippery banks. When tourist boats passed, they seemed to the villagers as big as <u>floating cities</u>. At nights their lights shone like <u>chandeliers</u>, seeming to offer a <u>palace of potential</u>. By day, the villagers rowed out in tiny boats, <u>water beetles</u> on the face of the river, to sell rolls of cloth. Often the tourists would ignore them, gazing across at the <u>tangled spider's web of vegetation</u> on the far bank.

5 and **6** Answers will vary.

Creating characters [p. 29]

1 clothes neat, shoes polished [a]　　furrowed brow [b]　　says little [d]　　speaks quietly [d] smiles a great deal [c]　　rarely makes eye contact [d]　　upright posture [a]　　leans forward to listen to others [c]　　taps to music [c]　　holds hands behind back [a] presses fingertips together [b] leans back in chair [c]　　rests chin on hand [b]

2 The speaker seems to be: a) prejudiced, b) bossy, authoritative, strict, c) exasperated, emotional

3
a) Relaxed, confident, dominant
b) Efficient, cool, collected, professional
c) Anxious, uneasy, unconfident or tense
d) Bullying, aggressive, angry

4
a) Ambition: wants professional and financial success
b) Wants approval/to please the man she is speaking to (son, husband?)
c) Wants power

5–7 Answers will vary.

Writing to describe [p. 34]

1 Answers will vary.

2 Possible answers:
a) A **solitary** cloud **drifts** across the sky like a **lost sheep**.
b) **Wearily**, the **overladen** train chugged through the **scorched** valley like a **late-summer caterpillar**.

3 Answers will vary.

4 Possible answers:
a) The <u>gaudy hot-air</u> balloon drifted <u>uncertainly</u> above the field of <u>chewing</u> cows.
b) A <u>bright</u> cloud of bluebells fills the wood, <u>their perfume hanging on the evening air</u>.

5–7 Answers will vary.

Writing to narrate [p. 35]

1–2 Answers will vary.

3

I hadn't touched my guitar for years, and it felt strange in my hands. Tentatively, I tried a chord of C, and was surprised to discover the instrument was almost in tune. I tweaked up the D-string a semitone and tried again: perfect.

4

Davina <u>wriggles</u> down the passage, the light from her head torch pooling just in front of her. <u>Is</u> it getting tighter, or <u>is</u> she just panicking?

'Come on,' <u>says</u> Molly. 'You can do it!'

'I can't,' she <u>sobs</u>. 'I'm going back.' But this <u>is</u> easier said than done. She <u>struggles</u> to hook her feet in the rock and pull back, but she <u>is</u> jammed tight.

5 and **6** Answers will vary.

CHAPTER 4 [pp. 38–50]

Deciding what is true or false [p. 38]

1
a) He warned that mechanical progress would eventually make people like brains in bottles.
b) producing charcoal for smelting iron
c) replacing destroyed habitats with new ones elsewhere
d) on the site of Smithy Wood
e) planting new trees

2 a), c), e), h)

3 b), d), e), f)

4 Monbiot makes his views about biodiversity offsetting clear through his choice of the word 'trash' to describe the removal of old woodland, and by his phrasing in paragraph four which makes a strong contrast between a valuable old oak tree and a young vulnerable 'sapling planted by a slip-road'. Monbiot suggests that restrictions have been relaxed due to the government's condition that 'more trees [should be] planted than destroyed' and through the interest that the service station company has since shown in Smithy Wood.

Summarising texts [p. 41]

1 In Steward's view the railway would ruin the natural beauty of the Thames valley.

2 There will be huge **disruption** to the landscape in the **area** of the railway, because of the structures that will be **necessary** to support it.

3 'local landowners are petitioning against the Bill'

4 Public enjoyment will be impaired, both on the river itself and in the surrounding area, natural views will be damaged, and Henley will lose its charm. The railway is unnecessary and not wanted by local people. All boating associations are opposed to it.

5 It is not possible to replace an ancient and historic natural habitat by creating a new one somewhere else.

6

	Source A (Monbiot)	Source B (Steward)
What each writer objects to	Proposal to build a motorway service station in place of Smithy Wood	New railway near Henley-on-Thames
Their reasons for objecting	Assumption that it is possible to compensate for a destroyed habitat by creating a new one elsewhere	Destruction of charm and natural beauty of the Thames and its valley
How hopeful they appear to be	Very little: final paragraph is bitter but resigned.	Convinced that everyone should see the railway is a bad idea: 'I need hardly point out …', 'unanimous', appeal to 'all-powerful aid' of newspaper.
What evidence you find for their views	'wiping out half the wood and fragmenting the rest', 'habitats you trash', 'reduced to a column of figures'	'disastrous', 'completely spoil', 'destroyed', 'healthy pleasure will be seriously interfered with'

7 Possible answer:

Both Monbiot and Steward are objecting to proposed commercial destruction of the natural environment: ancient woodland in the case of Monbiot, and the scenery of the Thames and its valley in the case of Steward.

Monbiot rejects the principle of 'biodiversity offsetting', which he defines as 'replacing habitats you trash with new ones created elsewhere'. He argues that Smithy Wood is beautiful and atmospheric, has a long history, and is part of local consciousness. It cannot be compensated for by rows of newly planted 'generic lines of saplings'. He also points out that the rules that once protected habitats from this approach have now been relaxed, so that habitats are under threat.

Whereas Monbiot gives several reasons for saving Smithy Wood, Steward sticks largely to one point – that the railway will spoil people's enjoyment of the existing scenery, and of the Thames, which he suggests deserves to be treated better because it is 'the Queen's highway'. He also points out that locals and river users are all opposed to it.

Monbiot seems to be bitterly resigned to the destruction of habitats by 'biodiversity offsetting', and nature being 'reduced to a column of figures', whereas Steward is much more hopeful that his campaign, with the paper's help, will succeed.

Understanding persuasive language [p. 45]

1

a) positive, respectful, appreciative

b) angry, incredulous (disbelieving), shocked, critical

2 angry, critical , annoyed, indignant

3 The tone becomes more militant and campaigning, with the listing of rowing associations that are 'unanimous against the scheme' and who have 'condemned' it, implying that the writer has a great deal of support and that no right-minded person would disagree with him.

4

Device	Definition	Example
Tricolon (triple, triad)	**Using three words or phrases in a row, often with the most powerful coming last**	… the accusation is groundless, dishonest, and libellous.
Rhetorical question	Question making a point rather than seeking an answer	Is that the best they can offer?
Alliteration	**Repeated use of consonant sounds, especially at the start of words**	This is cold comfort at best.
Parallelism	Achieving contrast by repeating a grammatical form	They claim that space exploration offers hope and inspiration; actually it **offers bankruptcy and disaster.**
Simile	Image comparing two things using 'like', 'as' or 'than'	**The river coiled like a snake through the lowlands.**
Metaphor	**Image comparing two things by speaking of one as if it were the other**	Samuel ploughed through his homework.

Device	Definition	Example
Personification	Giving human or godlike qualities to something abstract	Our patriotism is sleeping for now, but soon it will awake!
Juxtaposition	Presenting two contrasting things close together for effect	I exchanged my luxury en suite apartment for a **tin-roofed shack with a bucket for a toilet.**

5

a) triple (triad, pattern of three)

b) It gives a powerful sense of completion, as if the arguments cannot now be rejected.

6

a) alliteration – makes the idea sound ridiculous

b) metaphor – implying that the wood 'carries' the stories of local people, and perhaps even that these stories are going somewhere, like a freight train

c) repetition of words and form emphasises their connection – he sees them both as part of the same loss of tradition and individuality caused by modern commercialism

7

a) suggests thoughtless and complete destruction

b) negative, because 'habitats' has good connotations, while 'trashing' something is ruining it in a mindless, irresponsible way

c) juxtaposes the noble and beautiful world of nature with a very dull abstract man-made creation

d) implies that it will be ruinous

e) 'healthy' makes the pleasure sound all the more innocent and justified

f) an innocent phrase, hard to argue with

8 Answers will vary.

Comparing viewpoints and techniques [p. 48]

1 Author A's view of village festivals is negative: he thinks there are too many, and tries to avoid them, whereas Author B loves their variety and sense of rural tradition, and thinks that they show the strength of community spirit.

2

a) 'Every insignificant little place'

b) It makes it seem that there are just too many festivals.

c) It is a metaphor, implying that there is more money than people know what to do with.

d) It suggests that people become involved in festivals for selfish reasons.

e) It is a dismissive summing-up of his attitude.

3

a) 'I'm lapping it up' implies that he is enjoying it, like a cat lapping up cream.

b) 'farmers have tilled for centuries' – 'tilled' is an old-fashioned word; 'centuries' suggests a long history.

c) It is a triple (triad, tricolon) suggesting the great range of interesting, colourful things going on.

d) 'like a daddy-long-legs' physically describes the clown on stilts; a daddy-long-legs is a summer insect found in the country.

e) This summing-up suggests that all the things described show this positive fact – a healthy community life.

4

a) 'intent on partying' suggests that the attitude is deluded, as if they are trying to ignore facts; 'symptom' suggests illness; 'imminent collapse of society as we know it'

b) 'What's not to like?'; 'Community spirit is alive and well in the British countryside.'

5

a) Monbiot quotes Orwell, makes it clear that he has actually been to Smithy Wood himself, has researched its history and talked to locals, and that he knows the political background to 'biodiversity offsetting'; Steward shows that he has found out what the planned railway entails (bridges, etc.) and cites all the boating associations that are on his side.

b) 'I need hardly point out'; 'unanimous'

c) 'unthinkable a few months ago. No longer.'

d) Monbiot: 'Among the trees you can imagine your way into another world.' Steward: 'Thames scenery'; 'spoil many of the views of the wooded hills'

e) Monbiot uses emotive words like 'trash' and bitter irony ('Who cares …'), whereas Steward's tone is indignant, and more reasonable (as shown in 'disastrous' and 'completely spoil'), rather than bitter.

f) Steward appeals to the 'all-powerful' newspaper; seems convinced that no one could actually want the railway. Monbiot seems resigned: 'this is the way it's going now.'

6 a) Monbiot 2 and 4; b) Steward 2 and 3

7 a) Monbiot 4 and 5; b) Steward 4

8 Monbiot with a depressing vision of a future in which nature is replaced by numbers; a baffled Steward asks why anyone would want the railway.

9 Content should include:

Source A: Introduction with Orwell quotation for

authority and to gain interest. Language and detail describing Smithy Wood positively, as something worth preserving. Emotive use of 'trash' in definition of 'biodiversity offsetting'. Ironic rhetorical questions to juxtapose ancient woodland with new saplings, and comparing this with prints and original paintings. Final negative vision of nature replaced by figures.

Source B: Knowledgeable details relating to railway plan – comparable with Source A, knowledge of Smithy Wood and background to biodiversity offsetting. Negative adjectives ('disastrous', 'objectionable'), but, unlike Source A, no attempt to paint a picture of the beauty that would be lost – just the very mild 'views of the wooded hills'. Triple list of losses – public pleasure, Thames use, Henley's charm. Campaigning tone in list of associations 'unanimous against the scheme'. Final appeal to the newspaper for help is more optimistic than Source A.

CHAPTER 5 [pp. 51–9]

Key conventions of persuasive texts [p. 51]

1 Answers will vary, but must match the examples.

2 Suggested answer:

Teenagers today are not children playing with simple toys: they are young adults coping with a complex world. Yet at school and in society they are treated like children – irresponsible children who have no thought for the future, children who cannot make sensible decisions, children who cannot be trusted with the fate of the nation. Do politicians think we magically become responsible at the age of 18? What a miraculous transformation!

3 Suggested answers:

a) The other day I was listening to three teenagers in the lunch queue. What were they talking about? Pokémon GO? Man United? No, they were discussing the school kitchen's impact on the environment.

b) A staggering 87 per cent of teenagers are unable to name the current prime minister.

c) A recent study carried out by the University of Birmingham found that giving young people responsibility actually made them more responsible.

4

I often hear teenagers discussing political issues, even though they may not identify them as such. For example, the cost of school uniform is, in my view, a political issue.

You see graffiti scrawled on underpass walls and you probably assume this is just pointless vandalism. But you could see it as a demand for a voice in society. As

students, we ask you to consider us as near-adults who will become the future of our society. Society as a whole needs to see us as such, before we come to regard politics as boring and irrelevant.

5 Suggested answer:

Every £5 you donate will help to preserve **a natural habitat** for orphaned **elephants** like **Toto**. Every **baby elephant** deserves a **chance in life**. Give generously now, before it's **too late**.

6 Answers will vary.

Using persuasive language [p. 54]

1 Article for broadsheet newspaper b)
Letter to headteacher c)
Speech to teenagers of similar age a)

2 I am <u>furious</u> about the <u>disgraceful</u> state of facilities for the disabled. It is <u>completely unacceptable</u> that we have allowed this <u>shameful</u> situation to arise. I <u>strongly urge you</u> to consider how things can be improved for everyone concerned. It would be <u>wonderful</u> if all schools were properly resourced by the end of the year.

3 Answers will vary.

4 I had a terrible shock the other day: I tried to buy a ticket for a top football game at the weekend. The price? An unbelievable £55! Ridiculous. For that I could spend a night in a B & B, buy a posh meal out for two, including drinks, or buy a fitness watch, or even a pair of designer glasses. A price like that – they must be joking, I thought.

5 Simile: 'like a virus slowly worming its way around the body, damaging the organs one by one.'

6 Possible answers: '… rather like the way sugary drinks attract wasps'; '… it is like a drug'.

7 Answers will vary.

Planning and structure [p. 57]

1 Answers will vary.

2 Order: *either* 1 h), 2 c), 3 i), 4 e), 5 f), 6 a), 7 g), 8 b), 9 d)

or 1 h), 2 c), 3 f), 4 a), 5 i), 6 e), 7 g), 8 b), 9 d)

3 Suggested answers:

c) Pets are a luxury the world cannot afford.

i) Dog-fouling on pathways and in parks is disgusting, as well as being a health hazard.

e) Many owners fail to control their dogs.

f) Our wild bird and small mammal populations are decimated by cats.

a) Pet owners releasing unwanted or overgrown pets into the wild poses a threat to native species.

g) Pet lovers argue that dog-walking keeps people fit.

b) They also claim that cats have a calming effect on their owners, and provide company for the elderly.

4 Human beings have evolved partly through their natural curiosity. **However**, it might be said that in the case of space exploration this is 'idle' curiosity. We really have no need to know what conditions are like on Mars. **Moreover**, even getting an unmanned craft there is hugely expensive, **added to which** there is a strong chance that it will not even be able to land, **in which case** the money will have been wasted.

5 Some people think that money spent on pets is extravagant, and that it would be better spent on solving world poverty. They claim, moreover, that dogs are a public nuisance, and that cats kill wild birds. Nonetheless, I think that pets are well worth the money they cost, because they bring such great benefits to their human owners. What's more, I think the negatives of pet ownership are exaggerated.

6 Answers will vary.

CHAPTER 6 [pp. 60–7]

Paper 1: Explorations in creative reading and writing [p. 60]

1 Possible answers:

- Mowgli wants to trap and kill Shere Khan.
- Shere Khan has just had a meal and a drink.
- Shere Khan is in a steep-sided ravine.
- Shere Khan will find it hard to escape.
- Mowgli wants to surprise Shere Khan.
- Mowgli and Akela are leading a herd of buffalo towards the ravine.
- Vines and creepers grow up the side of the ravine.

2 You could include:

- the pause before the main action – the reader 'breathes' as well as the buffalo
- 'We have him in the trap' creates anticipation
- 'sleepy snarl' alliteration connects the words – Shere Khan sleepy but still dangerous
- detail of peacock leaving in fear; 'screeching' appeals to sense of hearing
- Mowgli's order to Rama simple but dramatic ('Down, Rama, down!')
- another pause on brink, then speed picks up; 'pitched' suggests headlong fall, or pouring from a pitcher; 'spurting' also powerful, suggests the ground is moving swiftly, like water
- simile 'just as steamers shoot rapids' creates sense of speed, power and danger
- Rama's bellow like a battle cry

3 You could include:

- topic sentence announces plan, which is explained
- description of Shere Khan having just had a meal and a drink, and his being in a steep-sided ravine, makes us anticipate Mowgli's success, but there is

still enough danger to hold interest
- pause and slowing of action while buffalo (and reader) 'breathe'
- language conveys great rush of action as buffalo pour into ravine, followed by relief as the plan succeeds

4 You could include:

- Mowgli's almost triumphant anticipation of victory, addressing Shere Khan – 'Now thou knowest!'
- vivid language describing charging buffalo – metaphor 'torrent', like a river in flood; 'foaming', 'staring eyes whirled …'; further reference to 'floodtime'
- 'thunder' of hoofs is dramatically contrasted with Shere Khan's 'lumbered', showing his heaviness and inability to escape
- actual killing of Shere Khan is understated ('something soft')
- continued violent action indicated by verbs joined by 'and' – 'goring and stamping and snorting'
- 'Softly now, softly! It is all over' successfully brings action to a close

5 Answers will vary.

Paper 2: Writers' viewpoints and perspectives [p. 64]

1 True statements: A, C, E, F

2 Answers should include:

Source A

- raises question of 'punishment and deterrence' or 'rehabilitation', and whether prisoners should have 'basic luxuries'
- points out that UK spends more on prisons than other countries yet has an inefficient system with overcrowding, with a high level of reoffending
- points out that, as in Norway, a more liberal system can result in more rehabilitation

Source B

- also says that prison does not work – high levels of reoffending
- says society has a duty to the criminal to rehabilitate them, and may need to do this by apparently harsh means: 'To be kind it is sometimes needful to be cruel.'
- argues that corporal punishment is more effective than prison, does not deprive families of the breadwinner, and would save money

3 Answers could include:

- use of simple statistics – '20, 30, and even 60 times'
- 'cure' and 'remedy' – implying that criminal is suffering from a disease, and can be rehabilitated
- analogy of medical operation – suggests that amputation is better than death by ineffective medicines; early 'cure' by corporal punishment is better than allowing criminal to become worse

ANSWERS

and eventually be killed
- strong adjectives criticising objections – 'sentimental and fallacious'
- triple driving home argument in 'most natural, Scriptural, and effective'
- ends on positive note – 'vast number of men restored and made good citizens'

4 Answers could include:

Source A
- much more open-ended in approach, initially presenting debate as a question – punishment v. rehabilitation
- mimics attitude of the pro-punishment argument in phrase 'wander from classroom to games room', as if prisoners have an easy time
- uses more detailed statistics to show extent of imprisonment and reconviction rates; quotes expert James Bell in support of her case
- anticipates critics in weak phrase 'unruly and dangerous behaviour' and then undermines using example of Bastøy Prison
- quotes Prison Radio Association and 'Michael' as evidence
- definite pro-rehabilitation message at end – the results of 'granting [prisoners] more responsibility are clear'

Source B
- emphasis in ideas and language on crime as a disease and society having a responsibility to the criminal to effect a 'cure'
- alliteration creates emphasis in 'confinement does not cure criminals, we are cruel and culpable in continuing' – crisp, decisive tone underlining idea that being soft on criminals is actually 'cruel'
- use of extended analogy of operation – approach based more on hypothetical narrative than on evidence; his statistics are vague and he does not quote actual cases, or quote criminals or experts
- irony in paraphrasing what a judge might say, echoing what he sees as the law's inconsistency – 'Still his body must not be touched'
- rhetorical question – 'Would it not be wiser …?'
- does cite opposing views, but quickly dismisses them
- overall approach much more single-minded and rhetorical than Source A, using the extended analogy, alliteration to suggest cruelty, and triples to drive home the argument

5 Answers will vary.

PART THREE: GCSE ENGLISH LITERATURE [pp. 68–100]

CHAPTER 7 [pp. 68–79]

How to use quotations [p. 68]

1
a) 'seemed colder than the clearer air'
b) 'candles […] faintly troubled its darkness'
c) 'oppressive'
d) 'as if a feast had been in preparation'
e) 'covered with dust and mould, and dropping to pieces'; 'cobwebs'

2
a) humour
b) appeal to the senses
c) personification
d) simile
e) alliteration
f) metaphor

3
a) Natural 'daylight' is 'completely excluded'.
b) The room, as shown by the grate, is 'old-fashioned'.
c) The narrator, Pip, may wish he was in the 'marsh mist' of his marshland home.
d) Dickens hints that the room was abandoned when 'a feast had been in preparation'.
e) The candlelight 'faintly troubled' the room, making it seem more gloomy.

4 Austen's comment that it is 'universally acknowledged' that a wealthy single man 'must be in want of a wife' is amusingly ironic, as it suggests that the narrator must believe this fact herself. This captivating opening line indicates that the main themes of *Pride and Prejudice* will be money and marriage.

5 Possible answer: The grand language used in Frankenstein's claim that he will 'unfold to the world the deepest mysteries of creation' shows how proud and ambitious he is. He evidently believes that he is capable of godlike knowledge, and that he seeks it for the benefit of mankind.

Key themes, contexts and settings [p. 71]

1 b), d) and e) could be themes. (a) Liverpool, although a setting, could also be a theme.)

2

Theme	Shakespeare play	Nineteenth-century novel
Kingship	✓	
Science and technology		✓

Theme	Shakespeare play	Nineteenth-century novel
Love and marriage	✓	✓
The supernatural	✓	✓
Education		✓
Revenge	✓	✓
Loyalty	✓	✓
Family dishonour	✓	✓
Poverty and working conditions		✓
Class inequality		✓

3 In 'Macbeth', Shakespeare **explores** the theme of the **supernatural** through the Witches' predictions and the appearance of Banquo's ghost to Macbeth. In the Witches, the **supernatural** is seen as **unreliable**, because they trick Macbeth with half-truths – for example, that he cannot be killed by 'man of woman born'. In Banquo's ghost, the **theme** is **linked** to Macbeth's sense of **guilt**, because only he can see the ghost. Yet even he cannot be sure of its reality, calling it an 'Unreal mockery'. A modern **audience** might be even more **inclined** to see it in **psychological** terms.

4 Shakespeare plays (S): a), c), d), f), i), l)

Nineteenth-century novels (N): b), e), g), h), j), k)

5 b), e), h), a), c), g), f), d)

Golding was writing in the 1950s, not long after the Second World War, in which he had served in the Navy. The rise of Hitler, the war and concentration camps had shown the human capacity for savagery, persecution of minorities, and the conflict in politics between democracy and dictatorship. In 'Lord of the Flies', Ralph represents a democratic leader, but one who lacks the charismatic appeal of Jack, whose hunting appeals more to many of the boys. The novel also reflects the Cold War, when it was feared that there could be a nuclear war because of the very different ideologies of the Communist USSR and the West. It is an imagined nuclear war that leads to the boys being marooned without adults on the island.

6 Not related to setting: e), h), i)

7 Answers will vary.

Writing about characters [p. 74]

1

a) money, parenthood
b) appearance and reality
c) appearance and reality, marriage, dishonour
d) destiny/fate
e) magic, power

2 It is the only time that a character can be guaranteed to speak honestly.

3 Answers will vary.

4 Modern plays often give **more** character-revealing stage directions than Shakespeare. However, both follow a pattern in which characters face **challenges** which eventually lead to a **resolution**. One important thing to establish in both a Shakespeare play and a modern play is each character's **motivation**.

5

a) storytelling from the point of view of one character, using 'I'
b) storytelling from the author's viewpoint, using 'he/she'
c) as for b), but seeing inside one character's head (e.g. 'How she hated this waiting!')
d) a first-person narrator who may give a biased view of events, reflecting their own character
e) a third-person viewpoint in which the author assumes total knowledge of all the characters, including their thoughts

6 At first, Scrooge is mean and self-centred. **[Point]** Even in midwinter he only has 'a very small fire', but he makes his clerk, Bob Cratchit, work with one so small 'that it looked like one coal'. He also threatens Cratchit with dismissal if he goes to put more coal on his fire. **[Evidence]** He is too mean to spend more money on coal, even to warm himself. This meanness over the fire symbolises Scrooge's lack of emotional warmth. **[Analysis]** I feel that this symbol works well because it appeals to the senses and readers can easily relate to it. **[Evaluation]**

7 Answers will vary.

Key literary techniques [p. 75]

1

a) simile – makes the fire seem alive and fast-moving
b) metaphor – reflects the shape and hardness of her beehive hairdo, and her defensiveness as a character
c) metaphor – makes him seem utterly ruthless, prepared to crush the child rather than stop or walk round her
d) simile – makes him seem in her power; shows she thinks she is superior to him

2

a) makes the night seem peaceful, romantic, enchanted
b) makes death and the hell of the enemy guns seem like devouring monsters
c) as if the winds are deliberately cruel and murderous, as well as painfully sharp
d) as if the stars are heaven's light, peeping (like a child?) through the dark sky; he does not want

goodness to prevent her acting evilly

3 c), a), f), e), b), d)

In *Pigeon English* the narrator, Harrison, becomes very attached to a pigeon, which he tries to feed on his balcony. The pigeon could be seen as symbolising hope, freedom, peace, or escape from the threat of gang violence.

4 When **Macbeth** speaks the line 'Is this a **dagger** which I see before me', he is **unsure** whether it is real or just 'A dagger of the mind'. For the **audience**, however, it is a **symbol** of the **temptation** Macbeth feels to carry out what he has planned with his wife: the **murder** of his king, Duncan. The imagined dagger could **represent** his desire to feel that he is being led, as if by fate, towards the murder, because he cannot at this point take **responsibility** for it.

5 b)

6

a) *Not a moment could be lost*: indicates great urgency

heaved: shows they are heavy, but she has to manage

deluged: indicates a large volume of water being poured

flew: shows she moves as quickly as she can

baptised: poured more water on, but hints that she is virtuous – linking to 'by God's aid'

devouring: the fire is like a hungry monster

b) The sentence is a long list of actions Jane performed, one after the other, using vigorous verbs. It comes to a climax with the long final phrase. The sentence shows what a great deal of rapid effort she had to make to put the fire out.

CHAPTER 8 [pp. 80–5]

Shakespeare [p. 80]

1

a) Shakespeare's plays are **mostly** in blank verse.
b) Commoners in Shakespeare generally speak in **prose**.
c) Blank verse means verse with no **rhyme**.
d) A line of blank verse normally has **five** pairs of syllables.
e) A scene often ends with a rhyming **couplet**.
f) Blank verse is written in **iambic** pentameter.

2 True statements: a), d), f)

3

a) personification and metaphor
b) the future
c) human life, and possibly his wife's life in particular
d) life – makes it seem meaningless

4

a) metaphor for death
b) Juliet's eyes are the sea, her body the 'bark'/ship, and her sighs the winds.
c) an extended metaphor
d) If she does not does not calm herself and stop crying, she will become ill.
e) England was a seafaring and trading nation; ships were often lost in storms.
f) Answers will vary, but he is essentially appealing to reason, using an elaborate poetic metaphor that is unlikely to be of much comfort to his grief-stricken daughter.

5 Answers will vary.

Nineteenth-century novels [p. 83]

1 a), b), c) (though very late in the nineteenth century), d), f), g), h)

2

a) It is the actions of others around us, in other words social conditioning, that make people bad.

b) Human beings are inevitably a mixture of good and evil

3

a) Marriage was tied up with money, especially in Austen's time (early nineteenth century). The eldest son inherited all the family wealth on the death of his father. Younger sons did not inherit, so they tried to marry into it.

b) There was widespread poverty and deprivation, and no social services to take care of orphans or neglected children. Some turned to crime in order to survive. They could be sent to prison at an early age, and usually reoffended on being released. Punishments were harsh. There was little concept of prison as rehabilitation.

c) Divorce was almost impossible, and was certainly socially unacceptable. An unhappy couple either stayed together or, less often, lived separately, but for one of them to live with someone else, unmarried, was considered immoral.

4 Answers will vary.

CHAPTER 9 [pp. 86–91]

Modern prose [p. 86]

1

a) Dan's character is revealed through: his habitual expression; the language describing his entry; foregrounded narrative viewpoint ('Such selfish …'); his verbal and physical abuse of the dog; and his threatening, possibly sexist challenge to the woman.

b) third person, but with one character (the woman) foregrounded

2 b), d)

3 This passage uses a third-person omniscient (all-knowing) narrator, with access to the character's thoughts, but foregrounds the character in 'He must remember …' he is actually thinking, 'I must remember …'

4 He treats 'her' as an object. He is single-pointed. The 'steel-rimmed' spectacles imply that he is unfeeling. His 'bony hand like a police road block' suggests he is severe and confident in his authority. He has no interest in what the woman has to say. His speech is formal and 'impersonal' – professionally detached. He speaks almost as if the woman no longer exists. The 'speck' could symbolise his brushing her away as if she is a 'speck', a minor distraction.

5 Answers will vary, but some suggestions are:
- *Lord of the Flies*: b), e), f), g), n), p)
- *Animal Farm*: a), g), h), n)
- *Never Let Me Go*: a), b), c), d), e), h), i), j), l)
- *Anita and Me*: b), d), e), f), h), k), l), n)
- *Pigeon English*: f), g), j), k), l)
- *Telling Tales*: f), k), o), p)

6 Answers will vary.

7 Answers will vary.

Modern drama [p. 89]

1 Answers will vary.

2 b), a), e), d), c)

3 Answers will vary.

4
a) Dramatic irony
b) Answers will vary.
c) An audience may feel drawn into the action because they feel that a secret has been shared with them.

5 a), b), d)

6 Answers will vary.

7
a) Birling is not only implying that he is important in the community, but also that he has influence and expects compliance from the Inspector. Birling's manner implies condescension, with an undertone of bullying.
b) 'I was an alderman for years … Bench' (I am a very important person in the community.)
'I know the Brumley police officers pretty well' (The police take note of what I say, so I expect you to.)
c) Answers will vary.

8 Answers will vary.

CHAPTER 10 [pp. 92–100]

Section B: Poetic techniques [p. 92]

1
a) *'My <u>name</u> is <u>Ozyman</u>dias, <u>king</u> of <u>kings</u>:*
<u>Look</u> on my <u>works</u>, ye <u>Mighty</u>, <u>and</u> de<u>spair</u>!'
In 'Ozymandias' the lines sound strong and confident. The iambic rhythm in the first line is varied in the second, forcing an emphasis on 'Look', so that it sounds like the pharaoh's command.
b) *<u>Slowly</u> our <u>ghosts</u> drag home: <u>glimps</u>ing the <u>sunk</u>*
fires, glozed
With <u>crusted</u> <u>dark</u>-red <u>jewels</u>; <u>crickets</u> <u>jing</u>le there
In 'Exposure', the rhythm of the first line drags along: it is impossible to speak it quickly. The second line changes, emphasising the value of home (what the men are fighting for). Alliteration joins with rhythm to emphasise the two most important words: 'jewels' and 'jingle'.

2
a) A line of poetry consisting of five iambic feet. A foot usually has one stressed and one unstressed syllable. Iambic is an unstressed syllable followed by a stressed one.
b) 'Porphyria's Lover', Sonnet 29, 'The Farmer's Bride', 'Ozymandias', 'London', *The Prelude*, 'My Last Duchess', 'Storm on the Island'

3
a) Two stresses per line:
The <u>dew</u> of the <u>morn</u>ing
Sunk <u>chill</u> on my <u>brow</u> –
It <u>felt</u> like the <u>warn</u>ing
Of <u>what</u> I feel <u>now</u>
b) ABAB
c) A depressed, sorrowful mood. The rhythm expresses disappointment in love. The short, end-stopped lines make the poem seem tight, closed off rather than expansive – like the relationship. The full rhymes at the end of lines also emphasise the sense of finality.

4
a) 'wire' and 'war' (perhaps also 'here'); 'brambles' and 'rumbles'
b) They create a sense of uneasiness and incompletion.

5 Extract a) begins with a metaphor, describing her thoughts as if they were ivy (or wild vines) growing round a tree, then explains the metaphor, turning it into a simile with 'as'. It suggests that her lover (husband) inspires her thoughts, and that she is central to her: her thoughts are twining round him, not the reverse.
Extract b) uses personification. The mountain is personified as having instinctive willpower, and a

head that it can raise up when it chooses. This has the effect of making nature seem alive, powerful and even threatening.

6

a)   *her cheek once more*
Blushed bright beneath my *burning* kiss:
        I propped her head up as *before*

In 'Porphyria's Lover', the 'b' alliteration creates a sense of explosive fullness, as if the dead woman is still bursting with life.

b) *In every voice, in every ban,*
The mind-forg'd manacles I hear

In 'London', 'mind' and 'manacles' are linked by alliteration, reinforcing the idea that the human mind, potentially wonderful and free, can create imprisoning chains – mental and physical. ('Ban' probably refers to the 'banns' read before a marriage, but it also suggests constraint, exclusion.)

7 Answers will vary.

Section C: Reading an unseen poem [p. 95]

1 'Black Forest' (south-west Germany)

2 'almost night'. The approaching night makes the experience more intense, and also has the visual effect of making the lightning more visible – increasingly so as the sky become fully dark.

3 'pure white liquid fire […] tipples over and spills down' (sheet lightning?) (1); 'a still brighter white snake' (fork lightning) (2); 'heavens cackle with unicorn sounds' (crackling thunder) (3); 'rain won't come' (the storm does not 'break' into rain) (4). Lawrence presents the absence of rain with astonishment. It is frustrating, but it creates a sense of the electric power still building up, tensely contained without the release of rain.

4 Lawrence concludes that, although human beings think they are clever in having 'mastered' electricity and other aspects of nature, in reality nature is beyond their control, and far more powerful than humankind.

5 'jugfull' (metaphor) suggests milk being poured endlessly – a sense of plenty, and perhaps sustenance (milk). 'Tipples' extends this metaphor.

'liquid fire' is, loosely, a metaphor, since fire cannot be liquid. It is also an oxymoron – an arresting juxtaposition of opposites. The phrase 'electric liquid' is similar: it seems like liquid, but it is not.

'white snake' describes wriggling lightning; it also suggests that the lightning is alive and full of energy, and perhaps dangerous.

'the heavens cackle with unicorn sounds' combines personification, as if the heavens are laughing (like a

witch?) at the human world, and the strange metaphor of 'unicorn sounds'. No one knows what unicorns sound like – they are mythical, so Lawrence may be: a) conveying a sense of the fairy-tale, magical wonder of the storm, and b) suggesting that the 'wriggling' white lightning is like a spiralling unicorn's horn.

'the rain refuses': personification, as if the rain has a mind of its own.

'chained': metaphor, implying vain human attempts to restrict nature.

6 'bronzey' is unusual, and delicate; 'gold-bronze' makes this more special, valuable; 'white liquid fire, bright white' seems pure, but also like milk; 'white snake' is arresting; unicorns are also white, suggesting purity.

7

a) Answers will vary.
b) Overall, they make the lightning seem alive and full of uncontrollable energy.

8 They sound heavy, reflecting the sense, but they are also ironic, since Lawrence is saying that humans certainly have not been able to do this. They all suggest slavery and brutal oppression – which humans have attempted to impose on nature, without success.

9 Repetition of 'jugfull', 'white', 'wriggles/wriggling' all suggest the never-ending power of nature and the effect of the storm as experienced by Lawrence; repetition of 'supposed to' emphasises the fact that humans think they have more power than they actually do.

10 Answers will vary, but should ideally include the points made in the answers above.

Sections B and C: Comparing poems [p. 98]

1 a)

'When We Two Parted': Romantic love; Separation, loss; Memory and time

'Love's Philosophy': Romantic love

'Porphyria's Lover': Romantic love; Separation, loss

Sonnet 29 – 'I think of thee!': Romantic love

'Neutral Tones': Romantic love; Separation, loss; Memory and time

'Letters from Yorkshire': Separation, loss; Memory and time

'The Farmer's Bride': Romantic love; Separation, loss

'Walking Away': Separation, loss; Family love; Memory and time

'Eden Rock': Family love; Memory and time

'Follower': Family love; Memory and time

'Mother, any distance': Separation, loss; Family love

'Before You Were Mine': Family love; Memory and time

'Winter Swans': Romantic love; Separation, loss

'Singh Song!': Romantic love

'Climbing My Grandfather': Family love

b)

'Ozymandias': Political power; Death, loss

'London': War, soldiers; Political power; Death, loss

'Extract from *The Prelude*': Nature; Inner conflict

'My Last Duchess': Political power; Death, loss

'The Charge of the Light Brigade': War, soldiers; Patriotism; Death, loss

'Exposure': War, soldiers; Patriotism; Death, loss

'Storm on the Island': Nature

'Bayonet Charge': War, soldiers; Patriotism

'Remains': War, soldiers; Death, loss; Inner conflict

'Poppies': War, soldiers; Patriotism; Death, loss; Inner conflict

'War Photographer': War, soldiers; Death, loss; Inner conflict

'Tissue': Political power

'The Emigrée': Political power; Death, loss

'Checking Out Me History': Political power; Patriotism

'Kamikaze': War, soldiers; Patriotism; Nature; Inner conflict

2 Possible comparisons:
a) 'Porphyria's Lover' – 'The Farmer's Bride', 'When We Two Parted'
   'Eden Rock' – 'Follower', 'Mother, Any Distance'
b) 'Ozymandias' – 'My Last Duchess', 'London'
   'Bayonet Charge' – 'The Charge of the Light Brigade'; 'Exposure'

3
a) Armitage focuses on the enduring connection between him and his mother, her hanging on to the tape measure (like an umbilical cord) as if supporting but also holding him back. Duffy focuses more on the mother herself, and what her life must have been like before motherhood.
b) Armitage's imagery of open country and astronauts suggest the freedom of detachment from his mother, but also abandonment anxiety. She is the metaphorical anchor securing him as a kite that can sail, but is still attached. The end of the poem pictures him as a fledgling bird, conveying his mixed feelings about freedom. Duffy's language

shows that she admires her mother, comparing her with Marilyn Monroe: her mother is associated with dance halls, fun and fashion.

4
a) 'Remains' is told in the first person, and in the present tense, in what could be the language of an ordinary soldier recounting an incident and his obsessive inability to forget it. It is as if we break into his story halfway through. 'War Photographer' is in the third person, and in the present tense, as if the poet is looking over the photographer's shoulder in the privacy of his darkroom. His feelings are expressed through observations, such as his shaking hands.
b) The soldier is damaged, unable to rid himself of the memory of killing a looter, even when he tries to numb himself with alcohol and drugs. The photographer is traumatised by his experiences, though at one level he has become unfeeling. He feels his job is necessary, yet has no lasting effect on magazine readers.

5
a) Answers will vary, but the repetition draws attention repeatedly to the 600 men. The sound of the rhymes also echoes the thundering of cannons.
b) This could be intended to make the colonial lesson sound childish and trivial.

6
a) 'When We Two Parted' is written in the past tense, fitting the sense of loss; 'Singh Song!' uses present tense, reflecting immediacy and the fact that the relationship is alive and well.
b) Stanza 1 of 'When We Two Parted' is halting and sad; stanza 3 of 'Singh Song!' is like a happy song (reflecting the pun in the title).
c) In 'When We Two Parted', rhymes contrast and connect words, as in 'fame' and 'shame'; 'Singh Song!' creates a sense of fun in unexpected rhymes (lines 3 and 5).

7
a) 'Neutral Tones' uses the bird simile to give a sense of something fleeting; 'Winter Swans' uses the iceberg metaphor to suggest coolness and separation, but also hidden depths and purity, and the boat simile to convey the idea that the lovers are recovering from an emotional upset.
b) 'Extract from *The Prelude*' uses personification to make the mountain sound powerful and threatening. The cat simile in 'Storm on the Island' is shocking, because we expect a pet to remain docile and harmless. It uses a metaphor to portray the wind as an enemy aircraft, the pilot attacking the island with machine-gun fire.

8 Answers will vary.